HANDEL

AMS PRESS
NEW YORK

GEORGE FREDERICK HANDEL.
(From a Portrait by Mercier in the possession of the Earl of Malmesbury.)

HANDEL

BY

ROMAIN ROLLAND

TRANSLATED BY

A. EAGLEFIELD HULL

MUS. DOC. (OXON.)

WITH AN INTRODUCTION BY THE EDITOR

WITH 17 MUSICAL ILLUSTRATIONS AND 4 PLATES

LONDON
KEGAN PAUL, TRENCH, TRUBNER & Co., Ltd.
BROADWAY HOUSE, 68–74 CARTER LANE, E.C.
1916

Reprinted from the edition of 1916, London

First AMS EDITION published 1971

Manufactured in the United States of America

International Standard Book Number: 0-404-05388-2

Library of Congress Catalog Number: 75-151597

AMS PRESS INC.
NEW YORK, N.Y. 10003

PREFACE

FOR a proper appreciation of the colossal work of Handel many years of study and a book of some two hundred pages are very insufficient. To treat at all adequately of Handel's life and work needs a whole lifetime in itself, and even the indefatigable and enthusiastic Chrysander, who devoted his life to this subject, has hardly encompassed the task. . . . I have done what I could ; my faults must be excused. This little book does not pretend to be anything more than a very brief sketch of the life and technique of Handel. I hope to study his character, his work, and his times, more in detail in another volume.

ROMAIN ROLLAND.

CONTENTS

PLATES

INTRODUCTION

BY THE EDITOR

HERE in England we are supposed to know our
Handel by heart, but it is doubtful whether we do.
Who can say from memory the titles of even six of
his thirty-nine operas, from whence may be culled
many of his choicest flowers of melody ? M. Rolland
rightly emphasises the importance of the operas of
Handel in the long chain of musical evolution, and
it seems impossible for anyone to lay down his book
without having a more all-round impression than
heretofore of this giant among composers.

M. Saint-Saëns once compared the position of a
conductor in front of the score of a Handel oratorio
to that of a man who sought to settle with his family
in some old mansion which has been uninhabited
for centuries. The music was different altogether
from that to which he was accustomed. No nuances,
no bowing, frequently no indication of rate, and
often merely a " sketched-in " bass. . . . Tradition only could guide him, and the English, who
alone could have preserved this, he considers, have
lost it.

Can it be recovered to any extent, and, if so, how ?
Behind each towering figure of genius are to be

found numbers of eloquent men who prepared the way for him ; and amongst these precursors there is frequently discovered one who exercised a dominating influence over the young budding genius. Such an influence was exercised by Zachau on Handel, and M. Rolland rightly gives due importance to the consideration of this old master's teachings and compositions, a careful study of which should go far to supplying the right key to Handel's music. One of the great shortcomings in the general musical listener is a lack of the historical view of music. It is a long cry from Bach and Handel to Debussy and Scriabin, but we shall be all the better for looking well at both ends of the long musical chain which connects the unvoiced expression of the past with the vague yet certain hopes of the future.

No doubt we have hardly yet recovered from the false position into which we have all helped to place Handel. He was never the great Church composer which has been assumed for so long. Perhaps, rather, he leaned to the pagan side of life in his art. As Mr. Streatfeild says, " You can no more call the *Messiah* a work of art than you can call the *Book of Common Prayer* popular as a masterpiece of literature. . . . Handel the preacher is laid for ever in the tomb, but Handel the artist with his all-embracing sympathy for human things and his delight in the world around him lives for evermore." Handel has been greatly, almost wilfully, misrepresented; but he has played too great a part in the history of English music to be cast aside on this account. It is true that there are many difficulties in the way of a clearer understanding of his music. A two-hundred years' overgrowth of vain vocal traditions is not going to be torn away in the space of a few years.

If the operas have been overlooked in favour of the oratorios, then his instrumental music has been even more neglected on account of the preponderance of his vocal movements. In a recent important contribution to Handelian biography only a few pages are given to the instrumental works. In this respect M. Rolland's clear and critical biography fills in a distinct *hiatus*.

Moreover, Handel sojourned in Germany, Italy, finally (and longest) in England—but never in France. M. Rolland, therefore, a Frenchman and the author of that brilliant work *Histoire de l'Opéra en Europe avant Lulli et Scarlatti*, may, more than any other writer, be expected to bring a freshness of vision and an impartial judgment to bear on Handel's works. *And he has not disappointed us.*

A. E. H.

GEORGE FREDERICK HANDEL

HIS LIFE

THE Handel family was of Silesian origin.[1] The grandfather, Valentine Handel, was a master copper-smith at Breslau. The father, George Handel, was a barber-surgeon, originally attached to the service of the armies of Saxony, then of Sweden, later of the French Emperor, and finally in the private service of Duke Augustus of Saxony. He was very rich, and purchased at Halle in 1665 a beautiful house, which is still in existence. He was married twice ; in 1643 he married a widow of a barber, who was ten years older than himself (he had six children by her) ; and in 1683, the daughter of a pastor who was thirty years younger than he was : he had four children by her, of which the second was George Frederick.

Both parents sprang from that good old *bourgeois*

---

[1] The genealogical tree of Handel has been prepared by Karl Eduard Förstemann : *Georg Friedrich Haendel's Stammbaum*, 1844, Breitkopf.

The name of Handel was very common at Halle in different forms (*Hendel, Hendeler, Händeler, Hendtler*). One would say that its derivation signified " merchant." G. F. Handel wrote it in Italian *Hendel*, in English and French *Handel*, in German *Händel*.

stock of the seventeenth century which was such excellent soil for genius and for faith. Handel, the surgeon, was a man of gigantic stature, serious, severe, energetic, religiously attached to duty, upright and affable in his dealings with those around him.

His portrait exhibits a large clean-shaven face which has the impression of one who never smiled. The head is carried high, the eyes morose ; prominent nose and a pleasant but obstinate mouth; long hair with white curls falling on his shoulders ; black cap, collar of lace, and coat of black satin : the aspect of a parliamentary man of his time.—The mother was no less sturdy a character. Of a clerical family on the maternal side as well as on the paternal side, with a spirit imbued with the Bible, she had a calm courage, which came out prominently when the country was ravaged by pestilence. Her sister and her elder brother were both carried off by the plague ; her father was also affected. She refused to leave them and remained quietly at home. She was then engaged to be married.—This sturdy couple transmitted to their distinguished son in place of good looks (which he certainly had not, and which never disquieted him) their physical and moral health, their stature, their keen intelligence and common sense, their application to work, and the indestructible essence of their quiet, calm spirit.

George Frederick Handel was born at Halle on Monday, February 23, 1685.[1] His father was then sixty-three years, and his mother thirty-four.[2]

The town of Halle occupied a singular political situation. It belonged originally to the Elector of Saxony ; by the Treaties of Westphalia it was ceded to the Elector of Brandenburg ; but it paid tribute to the Duke Augustus of Saxony during his lifetime. After the death of Augustus in 1680, Halle passed definitely to Brandenburg ; and in 1681 the Grand Elector came to receive homage there. Handel then was born a Prussian ; but his father was in the service of the Duke of Saxony, and he retained relationship with the son of Augustus, Johann Adolf, who moved his court after the Prussian annexation to the neighbouring town of Weissenfels. Thus the childhood of Handel was influenced by two intellectual forces : the Saxon and the Prussian. Of the two the more aristocratic, and also the more powerful was the Saxon. Most of the artists had emigrated with the Duke to Weissenfels. It was there that the genial Heinrich Schütz was born and died :[3] it was there that Handel found his first impetus, and where the calling of the child was first recognized. The precocious musical tendencies of the little George Frederick were somewhat curbed by the formal opposition of his

---

[1] It is interesting to note that Johann Sebastian Bach was born at Eisenach on March 21, 1685.

[2] Of the four children by the second marriage, the first died at birth. George Frederick had two sisters : one, two years, the other, five years younger than himself.

[3] He died in 1672.

father.[1] The sturdy surgeon had more than objection
—he possessed an aversion to the profession of artist.
This sentiment was shared by nearly all the sturdy
men of Germany. The calling of musician was
degraded by the unedifying spectacle of many
artists in the years of relaxation which followed the
Thirty Years' war.[2] Besides which, the *bourgeois*
German of the seventeenth century had a very
different idea of music from that of our French
middle classes of the nineteenth century. It was
with them a mere art of amusement, and not a
serious profession. Many of the masters of that
time, Schütz, Rosenmüller, Kuhnau, were lawyers,
or theologians, before they devoted themselves to
music ; or they even followed for a time the two
professions. Handel's father wished his son to
follow his own profession, that of law ; but a journey
to Weissenfels overcame all his objections. The
Duke heard the little seven-year-old Handel play
the organ, with the result that he sent for the father
to see him and recommended him not to thwart the
child's obvious musical talents. The father, who
had always taken these counsels very badly when
they came from anyone else, doubtless appreciated
them when they came from the lips of a prince ;

[1] Legendary anecdotes of the little Handel are often quoted,
showing him rising from his bed in the middle of the night to
play a little clavichord, which was concealed in an upper garret.
[2] See the Preface which the choirmaster of the Thomas School
at Leipzig, Tobias Michael, wrote to the second part of his
Musikalische Seelenlust (1637) ; and in the life of Rosenmüller
the story of the scandalous affair which in 1655 forced this fine
musician to flee from his country (August Horneffer : *Johann
Rosenmüller*, 1898).

and without renouncing his own right over his son (for he still had the legal plan in his head) consented to let him learn music ; and on his return to Halle he placed him under the best master in the town, the organist Friedrich Wilhelm Zachau.[1]

. . . . . .

Zachau was a broad-minded man and moreover a good musician, whose greatness was only appreciated many years after his death.[2] His influence on Handel was splendid. Handel himself did not conceal it.[3] This influence affected the pupil in two ways : by his method of teaching, and by his artistic personality. " The man was very well up in his art," says Mattheson,[4] " and is possessed of as much talent as beneficence."

. . . . . .

Handel's devotion to Zachau was so great that he seemed never able to show him sufficient affection and kindness. The master's first efforts were devoted to giving the pupil a strong foundation in harmony. Then he turned his thoughts towards the

[1] F. W. Zachau was born in 1663 at Leipzig, and died prematurely in 1712. His father came from Berlin. The original spelling of the name was *Zachoff*.

[2] Since the publication of the works of Zachau by Max Seiffert in the *Denkmäler deutscher Tonkunst*, Vols. XXI and XXII, 1905, Breitkopf.

[3] Matheson refers to this briefly also, but the later historians, Chrysander, Volbach, Kretzschmar, Sedley Taylor have not taken any account of these words, which they attribute to the generosity of Handel, and to the malevolence of Matheson. In their judgment he did not even know the works of Zachau— this is very hard on Handel's master. Since the publication of the *Denkmäler* it is impossible not to recognize in Zachau the true originator of his style, and even, so to speak, of the genius of Handel.   [4] *Lebensbeschreibung Haendels* (1761).

inventive side of the art ; he showed him how to give his musical ideas the most perfect form, and he refined his taste. He possessed a remarkable library of Italian and German music, and he explained to Handel the various methods of writing and composing adopted by different nationalities, whilst pointing out the good qualities and the faults of each composer ; and in order that his education might be at the same time theoretical and practical, he frequently gave him exercises to work in such and such a style.

. . . . . .

This education with a true European catholicity was not confined to one particular musical style, but spread itself out over all schools, and caused him to assimilate the best points of all, for who can fail to see that the conception and practice of Handel, and indeed the very essence of his genius, was the absorption of a hundred different styles ! " One of his manuscripts dated 1698, and preserved carefully all his life, contains," so says Chrysander, " some airs, choruses, capriccios, and fugues of Zachau, Alberti (Heinrich Albert), Froberger, Krieger, Kerl, Ebner, Strungk, which he had copied out whilst studying with Zachau." Handel could never forget these old masters, distinct traces of whom are found from time to time in his best-known works.[1] He would doubtless too, with

[1] One notices many of Kerl's themes in one of Handel's Organ concertos, and in a Concerto Grosso. A *canzone* of Kerl ; also a *capriccio* of Strungk has been transferred bodily into two choruses of *Israel in Egypt* (Max Seiffert: *Haendels Verhältnis zu Tonwerken ælterer deutscher Meister*, Jahrbuch Peters, 1907).

Zachau, have seen the first volumes of the clavier works of Kuhnau, which were published at that time.[1]

Moreover, it seems that Zachau knew the work of Agostino Steffani,[2] who later on took a fatherly interest in Handel ; and Zachau followed sympathetically the dramatic musical movement in Hamburg. Thus the little Handel had, thanks to his master, a living summary of the musical resources of Germany, old and new ; and under his direction he absorbed all the secrets of the great contrapuntal architects of the past, together with the clear expressive and melodic beauty of the Italian-German schools of Hanover and Hamburg.

But the personal influence of the character and the art of Zachau reacted no less strongly on Handel than did his methods of instruction. One is struck by the relationship of his works[3] to those of Handel ; they are similar in character and style. The reminiscences of motives, figures, and of subjects count for little ;[4] there is the same essence in the art

[1] The two parts of the Clavier Exercises of Kuhnau appeared in 1689 and 1692. The new Clavier Pieces in 1696 and the Bible Sonatas in 1700. (See the edition of Kuhnau's clavier works by Karl Pasler in the *Denkmäler deutscher Tonkunst*, 1901).

[2] See Chrysander. We shall speak later on of the work of Steffani and its relation to Handel.

[3] The volume of his published works comprises 12 cantatas for orchestra, soli, and chorus, and a *capella* (unaccompanied) Mass, a chamber work (trio for flute, bassoon, and continuo), 8 preludes, fugues, fantasias, capriccios for clavecin or organ, and 44 choral variations.

[4] Compare the Tenor air *O du werter Freudengeist* (p. 71) and accompaniment, and *ritornello* of the *violini unisoni* in the 4th cantata *Ruhe, Friede, Freud und Wonne* with the air of Polyphemus in Handel's *Acis and Galatea* ; compare also the subject in the Bass air of the 8th cantata (p. 189) with the well-known

of both master and pupil ; there is the same feeling
of light and joy ; there is nothing of the pious
concentration and introspection of Bach, who
goes down into the deeps of thought, and who
loves to probe into all the innermost recesses of
the heart, and—in silence and solitude—converse
with his God. The music of Zachau is the music
of great spaces, of dazzling frescoes, such as one
sees on the domes of the Italian cathedrals of the
sixteenth and seventeenth centuries ; but Zachau's
work contains more religion than these. His music
pulses with action like the bounding and rebound-
ing of great springs of steel. It has triumphant
subjects with expositions of great solemnity. There
are victorious marches, carrying everything before
them, which go crashing on without stopping, ever
spurring on the sparkling and joyous patterns.
There are also pastoral themes, pure and voluptuous
reveries,[1] dances, and songs accompanied by flutes,
with a Grecian perfume,[2] and a smiling virtuosity,
a joy intoxicated with itself, twisting lines, and
vocal arabesques, vocalizations, trills for the voice
which gambol light-heartedly with the little wave-
like arpeggios of the violins.[3] Let us unite these
two traits : the heroic and the pastoral, the warriors'
marches and the jubilant dances. There you have

instrumental piece which Handel used for the Symphony in the
Second Act of *Hercules ;* also the Tenor solo with horn, *Kommt
jauchzet* (p. 181) in the 8th cantata : *Lobe den Herrn, meine Seele*
with the soprano air in *The Messiah.* One also finds in the
cantata *Ruhe, Friede* (p. 83) the sketch for the famous chorus of
the destruction of the walls of Jericho in *Joshua.*

[1] *Ruhe, Friede,* p. 122.   [2] *Ibid.,* pp. 113, 183.
[3] *Ibid.,* pp. 110, 141, 254, 263.

the Handelian tableaux : the people of Israel and
the women dancing before the victorious army.
You find in Zachau a sketch for the monumental
constructions of Handel in his Hallelujahs ; those
mountains of sound which resound their joy, the
colossal *Amens* which crown his oratorios like the
dome of St. Peter at Rome.[1]

Add to this also Zachau's marked liking for
instrumental music,[2] which makes him combine it
so happily with the vocal solos ; and very often he
imagines the voice as an instrument, which com-
bines and gambols with the other instruments, thus
forming a decorative garland harmoniously woven.

[1] *Ibid.* 8th Cantata. *Lobe den Herrn, meine Seele*, p. 166,
the German *Hallelujah* with its fine flow of jubilant vocalizing—
especially on page 192, the great final chorus.

[2] See his pretty trio for flute, bassoon and clavier (p. 313).
It is a small work in 4 movements (1. *Affettuoso ;* 2. *Vivace ;*
3. *Adagio ;* 4. *Allegro*), where clear Italian grace mixes itself so
happily with German *Gemüth.*

The orchestra for the cantatas seldom includes anything
but the strings with the organ or the clavier. But in general the
palette of Zachau is very rich, comprising violas, violetti,
violoncello, harps, oboes, flutes, hunting horns, bassoons and
bassonetti, and even clarini (high trumpets) and drums (Cantata :
Vom Himmel kam der Engel Schar).

Zachau amuses himself by combining the tone-colours of the
different instruments with those of the voices in the solo airs ;
thus a Tenor air is accompanied by a violoncello solo ; another
by two hunting horns ; an air for the Bass is combined, with
the bassoon *obbligato ;* another with 4 drums and trumpets ; a
Soprano air with the bassoon and 2 bassonetti ; without
mentioning innumerable airs with oboes or flutes.

Thanks to Zachau, Handel was familiarized at an early date
with the orchestra. He learnt at his house how to play all the
instruments, especially the oboe, for which he has written many
charming numbers. When he was ten years old he wrote some
Trios for 2 oboes and bass. An English nobleman travelling in
Germany found a little collection of 6 Trios (Sammlung dreistim-
miger Sonaten für Zwei Oboen und Bass, sechs Stück) dating
from this period (Volume 28 of the Complete Handel Edition).

To sum up, it was an art less intimate than expansive, an art newly born ; not devoid of emotion though,[1] but above all, restful, strong, and happy—an optimistic music like that of Handel.

Truly Handel in miniature, with much less breadth, less richness of invention, and particularly a smaller power of development. There is nothing of the attractiveness of Handel's colossal movements, like an army which marches and sings ; and more solid strength is necessary to carry the weight right to the end without bending. Zachau flinches on his way ; he has not the vital force of Handel, but in compensation he has more *naïveté*, more tender candour, more of the childlike chasteness and evangelic grace.[2] Certainly there we have the master really necessary to Handel, a master more than one great man had the good fortune to find (it is Giovanni Santi for Raphael ; it is Neefe for Beethoven) : good, simple, straightforward, a little dull, but giving a steady and gentle light where the youth may dream in peace and abandon himself with confidence to a guide almost fraternal, who does not seek to dominate him, but rather strives to fan the little flame into a greater fire ; to turn the little rivulet of music into the mighty river of genius.

[1] See his beautiful air for bass in the Cantata *Lobe den Herrn*, p. 164.

[2] Certain very simple phrases as in the Cantata for the *Visitation*, " *Meine Seel erhebt den Herren*," the recitative for Soprano " *Denn er hat seine elende Magd angesehen* " (p. 112) have an exquisite flavour of virginal humility which we never find in Handel.

Whilst studying with Zachau the young Handel visited Berlin. After having paid his homage to his former master, the Elector of Saxony, he was wise enough also to present himself to the new one, the Elector of Brandenburg. It seems that this journey took place about 1696 when the boy was eleven years old, and his father, being ill, did not accompany him.

The Berlin Court lived a very short life of artistic brilliance between the wars of the Grand Elector and those of the Prince-Regent. Music was greatly in honour, thanks to the Electress, Sophia Charlotte, daughter of the celebrated Sophia of Hanover. She attracted to her the best Italian instrumentalists, singers, and composers.[1] She founded the Berlin Opera,[2] and even conducted several concerts at Court. Doubtless the movement was but superficial. It was only held together by the impulse of the Electress, who had more spirit than earnestness. Art was for her only a fond distraction ; so that after her death the musical *fêtes* in Berlin became extinct. But it was something to have lighted, only for a brief hour, this flame of beautiful Italian art, and it was thus that the little Handel came into contact for the first time with the music of the South.[3] The child, who displayed his powers

[1] The Torellian violinist, Antonio Pistocchi, who was one of the masters of Italian song, the father, Attilio Ariosti, Giovanni Bononcini, Steffani, who wrote for the Electress some famous duets, and Corelli, who dedicated to her his last Violin Sonata, op. 5.

[2] The first representation took place June 1, 1700, with a pastoral ballet of Ariosti. Leibnitz was present at the full rehearsal.

[3] All that one has heard of his meeting with Ariosti and Bononcini is somewhat legendary. A. Ebert has shown that

on the clavecin before a princely audience, had so much success that the Elector of Brandenburg wished him to enter his service. He offered Handel's father to send the child to Italy to finish his studies The old man refused. " He had a stubborn pride, and did not desire," so says Mainwaring, " that his son should be tied too soon to a Prince." He wished to see his child again, as he considered that he himself might die at any moment.

Little Handel returned. Too late ! He learnt *en route* that his father had died on February 11, 1697. The principal obstacle in the way of his musical vocation had now disappeared, but he had so profound a respect for his father's wishes that he forced himself to study law for many more years. After having completed in due course his classes at the college he was entered for the Faculty of Law at the University of Halle on February 10, 1702, five years after his father's death.

University life in Halle at that time was of a revolting character. But, in spite of this, an intense life of thought and religion was also to be found there. The Faculty of Theology was the centre of Pietism.[1] The students devoted themselves to

Ariosti only went to Berlin in 1697, and that Bononcini did not arrive in Germany till November, 1697, and they were not there together before 1702. In order that Handel should have met them there it was necessary that they should return in 1703 on their way to Hamburg. But then he was eighteen years ; and the legend of the infant prodigy being victorious over the two masters thus disappears (*Attilio Ariosti in Berlin*, 1905, Leipzig).

[1] The broad-minded policy of the Electors of Brandenburg attracted to their University at Halle many of the most independent men in Germany who had been persecuted elsewhere. Thus the Pietists who were driven from Leipzig came

religious exercises which led to ecstasy.—Handel, independent as he always was, kept clear of the brutal amusements, just as he did of the mystic contemplation. He was religious without being sentimental. For the rest, an artist could only listen to the Pietists with difficulty, for their religious devotion was too often oppressive to art. Even J. S. Bach, Pietist at heart, by his public acts declared himself opposed to the Pietists, who were on certain marked occasions inimical to music.[1] For a still stronger reason Handel had no leaning towards mysticism.

Religion was not his business; Law certainly was not. However, he had for his master the most remarkable professor in Germany, Christian Thomasius, the advocate in the arraignment of witchcraft,[2] the reformer of the teaching of law, who himself made a thorough study of German customs, and who did not cease to make battle with the gross and stupid abuses of the universities, with their spirit of caste, pedantry, ignorance, hypocrisy, and judicial and religious acerbity. If such a training was not of the nature to retain Handel it was certainly not the fault of the professor; there were no more vital lessons in the

---

to Halle. Indeed they flocked there from all parts of Germany, Switzerland, and the Low Countries (Volbach: *Vie de Haendel*, and Levy-Bruhl: *L'Allemagne depuis Leibnitz*, 1890).

[1] See the fine studies of J. S. Bach by Pirro.

[2] One knows that the trial of witchcraft was one of the many blots on this period. More than a hundred thousand victims perished in the funeral pyres of witchcraft in one century! Frederick II said that if women could die peacefully of old age in Germany, it was all owing to Thomasius.

whole of the Germany of that day ; none which offered a more fruitful field of activity to a young man. Let us be sure that a Beethoven would not have been insensible to them. But Handel was a pure musician ; he was music itself ; nothing else could occupy his thoughts.

In the year in which he had completed his terms in the Faculty of Law he found a post of organist at Halle : and in a church more than strictly Lutheran, being of the Reformed order, where the organist had expressly to conform to the new cult. However, he was only seventeen years old.[1] This simple fact showed what musical authority he already exercised in the town where he had studied law.[2] Not only was he organist, but he was also Professor at the College of the Reformists; he took vocal music there for two hours every week ; he selected the most gifted of his pupils and formed from them a vocal and instrumental body which was to be heard every Sunday in one church or another of the town. He included in his musical repertoire, chorales, Psalms, motets, cantatas—which were changed every Sunday. Truly an excellent school for learning to write quickly and well. Handel there formed his creative fecundity.[3] Of hundreds of cantatas which

[1] The yearly contract with the Cathedral church was dated March 30, 1702, a month after he had signed the faculty of law.

[2] Telemann, passing through Halle in 1701, said that he made the acquaintance of Handel, who was already there " a man of importance " (" Dem damahls schon wichtigen Herrn Georg Friedrich Haendel ")—a singular epithet indeed to apply to a child of sixteen years ! Chrysander had indeed reason to insist on the precocious maturity of Handel, " No one was his equal in that, even J. S. Bach, who developed much more slowly ! "

[3] Already for several years he had composed " like the devil," as he said of himself once.

he then wrote, none were preserved by him.[1] But it is certain that his memory retained more than one idea to serve in later compositions, for he never lost anything, and from that time for the rest of his life he retained in his mind his earlier musical ideas. This should not be attributed to his speed in working, but to the unity of his thought and his strenuous search for perfection.

Handel renewed neither his yearly engagement at the Cathedral of Halle nor at the University. In his period as organist he had gauged his own musical force and he no longer wished to constrain it. A wider field of activity was necessary. He quitted Halle in the spring of 1703, and guided both by his instincts and by a preference of his master Zachau[2] he betook himself to Hamburg, the city of German Opera.

Hamburg was the Venice of Germany. A free town far from the noise of wars, a refuge of artists, and people of large fortunes, the centre of the commerce of Northern Europe, a cosmopolitan city

[1] There are attributed to him two oratorios (very doubtful), one Cantata, *Ach Herr mich armen Sünder*, and a *Laudate Pueri* for Soprano solo, which are anterior to his departure for Hamburg.

[2] Alfred Heuss was the first to show what attraction the musical drama had for Zachau, who introduced it even into the Church. Some of his cantatas, the 4th, for example, *Ruhe, Friede, Freud und Wonne*, very unjustly criticised by Chrysander, is a fragment of a fantastic opera where one finds David tormented by evil spirits. The declamation is expressive, and the choruses have a highly dramatic effect. Thus we see the theatrical career of Handel was prepared in Halle, and perhaps it was Zachau himself who sent Handel to Hamburg (A. Heuss: *Fr. Wilh. Zachau als dramatischer Kantaten-Komponist*). (I.M.G., May, 1909).

where they spoke all languages and especially the French tongue, it was in continual relationship with both England and Italy, and particularly with Venice, which constituted for it a model for emulatation. It was by way of Hamburg that the English ideas were circulated in Germany. It was there where the first German newspapers appeared.[1] In the time of Handel, Hamburg shared with Leipzig the intellectual prestige of Germany. There was no other place in Germany where music was held in such high esteem.[2] The artists there hobnobbed with the rich merchants. Christoph Bernhart, pupil of Schütz, had founded there a celebrated Collegium Musicum, a Society of Musicians, and started there in 1677–8 the first theatre of German Opera. It was not a princely opera open only to those invited by the prince, but a public opera, popular in spirit and in prices. It was the example of Italy, notably that of Venice, which called forth this foundation, but the spirits of the two theatres were very different. Whilst that of Venice satisfied itself with fantastic melodramas, curiously devised from the ancient mythology and history, the Hamburg Opera retained, despite the grossness of taste and licentiousness of manners, an old religious

[1] In reality under the influence of English publications, and notably *The Spectator* of Addison, 1711. About 1713 *The Man of Reason* appeared in Hamburg. In 1724 to 1727 the journal *The Patriot* of Hamburg was founded by a patriotic society. The original intention was to print 400 copies, but 5000 were subscribed for in Upper Saxony alone.

[2] The secular music about 1728 reckoned in its ranks 50 masters and 150 professors. In comparison, religious music was much more poorly represented than in many other cities of north Germany.

foundation. The Hamburg opera was inaugurated in 1678 by the production of Joh. Theile's *Creation of the World*. The composer was a pupil of Schütz. From 1678 to 1692 a large number of religious dramas were given there; some of an allegorical character, others inspired by the Bible. In certain of these subjects one can already see the future oratorios of Handel.[1] Feeble as these pieces were, they were yet on the definite road for the founding of a real German theatre. It seems to have been the idea of one of these poets, Pastor Elmenhorst, who wished to give to the religious opera the value of a classic form of art.[2] Unfortunately, the public spirit was on the decline; its religious resources, however, were well protected, save in a minority where religion took a more aggressive character as it felt itself less able to hold people. There were two factions in the Hamburg public; one (the most numerous) whom religion bored, and who wished to amuse themselves at the theatre. The other party was religious and would not have anything to do with the opera under the impression that it was a work of Satan, *opera diabolica*.[3] The struggle was warmly contested between the two factions, and religious opera came to grief. The last representation took place in 1692. When Handel arrived it was truly the *opera diabolica* which ran with its many extravagances and its licentious habits.

---

[1] *The Birth of Christ, Michael and David, Esther.*
[2] *Dramatologia antigua-hodierna*, 1688.
[3] *Theatromachia*, or *die Werke der Finsterniss* (The Powers of Darkness), by Anton Reiser, 1682.

I have told elsewhere[1] the story of this period of theatrical history in Hamburg, of which the golden age was certainly between 1692 and 1703. Many conditions contributed to the establishment of a good Theatre and Opera at Hamburg ; money and the wealthy patrons disposed to expend it, an excellent band of instruments, good but small in number, a scenic art well advanced, a luxury of decoration and machinery, renowned poets, musicians of great value, and, rarest of all, the poets and musicians who assembled from " die sich wohl verstanden," as Mattheson wrote. The poets were named Bressand of Wolfenbüttel, who was inspired by the French theatre, and Christian Postel, whom Chrysander calls very complacently a German Metastasio. The feeblest part was the singing. For a long time the Hamburg Opera had no professional singers. The *rôles* were taken by students and artisans, by shoemakers, tailors, fruiterers, and girls of little talent and less virtue ; generally the artisans found it more convenient themselves to take the female *rôles*. Men and women alike had a profound ignorance of music. Towards 1693 the Opera at Hamburg was fortunately completely transformed from top to bottom by the great Kapellmeister Sigismund Cousser, who introduced reforms in the orchestra after the French model, and in the singing on Italian lines. France was represented in his eyes (as for all foreign musicians) by the personage of Lully, by whom Cousser was trained for six years in Paris. Italy

[1] *Histoire de l'Opéra avant Lully et Scarlatti*, 1895, pp. 217–222.

was represented by a remarkable artist settled at
Hanover from 1689 to 1696, who produced ten
operas ; Agostino Steffani from the province of
Venice.

This dual model from Italy and France, aided by
the personal example of Cousser, played the chief
part in producing the best musician of the Hamburg
Opera, Reinhärd Keiser, a man who, despite his
character and presumptuous knowledge, had
certainly genius.[1]

Keiser was under thirty years old when Handel
arrived, but he was then at the zenith of his fame.
Kapellmeister of the Hamburg Opera since 1695,
then director of the theatre since the end of 1702,
very highly gifted, but of scanty culture, dissipated,
voluptuous, careless, he was the incontestable ruler
of the German Opera ; the artist type of that
epoch, overflowing with material life, and devoting
itself to the love of pleasure. The influence of both
Lully[2] and that of Steffani[3] is shown in his first
operas. But his own personality is easily recog-
nizable under these traces of borrowing. He has a
very fine sense of instrumental colour, widely

[1] Reinhärd Keiser was born in 1674 at Teuchern, near
Weissenfels, and he died in 1739 at Copenhagen.
    See Hugo Leichtentritt: *Reinhärd Keiser in seinen Opern,*
1901, Berlin ; Wilhelm Kleefeld : *Das Orchester der ersten
deutschen Oper,* 1898, Berlin ; F. A. Voigt : *Reinhärd Keiser*
(1890 in the *Vierteljahrsschrift für Musikwissenschaft*)—the
Octavia and the *Croesus* of Keiser have been republished.
[2] For instance in the overtures in 3 parts, with French
indications " *Vitement, Lentement* " ; also in the instrumental
preludes, and perhaps in the dances.
[3] Principally in the duets, which have a slightly contrapuntal
character.

differing from that of the followers of Lully, who
were a little disdainful of expressive power in the
orchestra, and were always disposed to sacrifice it
to the primacy of the voice.[1] He believed, as did
his admirer and commentator, Mattheson, that one
can express the feelings by means of the orchestra
alone.[2]

He was, moreover, a true master of *recitative;* one might say that he created the German
recitative. He attached extreme importance to it,
saying that the expression in *recitative* often gave
the intelligent composer much more trouble than
the invention of the air.[3] He sought to note with
exactitude, accent, punctuation, the living breath
itself, without sacrificing anything of the musical
beauty. His *Recitative arioso* takes an inter-
mediate place between the oratorical *recitative* of
the French, and the *recitative secco* of the Italians,
and was one of the models for the *recitative* of J. S.

---

[1] " Is it the orchestra which is the hero ? " asked the theorist
of Lullyism, Lecerf de la Viéville. " No, it is the singer. . . ."
" Oh, well, then, let the singer move me himself, and take care
not to worry me with the orchestra, which is only there by
courtesy and accident. *Si vis me flere. . . .*" (*Comparaison de la
Musique italienne et de la Musique française,* 1705).

[2] " One can represent quite well with simple instruments,"
says Mattheson, " the grandeur of the soul, of love, of jealousy,
etc., and render all the feelings of the heart by simple chords and
their progressions without words, in such a way that the hearer
can know and understand their trend, the sense and thought of
the musical discourses as if it were a veritably spoken one " (*Die
neueste Untersuchung der Singspiele,* 1744).

[3] The preface of the *Componimenti Musicali* of 1706. Mattheson exaggeratingly says that " to compose well a single recitative
in keeping with the feelings and the flow of the phrase as Keiser
did, needs more art and ability than to compose ten airs after
the common practice."

Bach,[1] and even not excepting Bach and Handel, Mattheson persists in seeing in Keiser the master of this style.—But the real supreme gift of Keiser was his melodic invention. In that he was one of the first artists in Germany, and the Mozart of the first part of the eighteenth century. He had an abundant and winning inspiration. As Mattheson said, " His true nature was tenderness, love. . . ." From the commencement to the end of his career he could reproduce voluptuous feelings with such exquisite art that no one could surpass him. His melodic style, much more advanced than that of Handel— not only at this particular epoch but at any moment of his life—is free, unsophisticated and happy. It is not the contrapuntal style of Handelian Opera, but it inclines rather to that of Hasse (who was trained entirely in it), to the symphonists of Mannheim, and to Mozart. Never has Handel, greater and more perfect as he was, possessed the exquisite note which breathes in the melodies of Keiser—that fresh perfume of the simple flower of the field.[2] Keiser had the taste for popular songs and rustic scenes,[3] but he knew also how to rise to the very summits of classical tragedy, and some of his airs of

[1] Compare the *recitative* in the first great cantatas of J. S. Bach, " Aus der Tiefe, Gottes Zeit," which cover from 1709 to 1712–14, with such *recitatives* from " Octavia " of Keiser (1705), notably Act II, *Hinweg, du Dornen schwangre Krone !* Melodic inflections, modulations, harmonies, grouping of phrases, cadences, all in the style of J. S. Bach even more than in that of Handel.

[2] See in *Croesus* (1711) the air of Elmira, with flute, which calls to mind a similar air from *Echo and Narcissus* by Gluck.

[3] In this genre a scene from *Croesus* is a little masterpiece in the pastoral style of the end of the eighteenth century ; and is very close to Beethoven.

stately grief might have been written by Handel
himself.[1] Keiser was, then, full of lessons and of
models for Handel, who was not slow to take them,[2]
but he also set him several bad examples too. The
worst was the renunciation of the national language.
Whilst Postel and Schott had been at the head of
the Hamburg Opera the Italian language had been
kept within bounds,[3] but since Keiser had become
Director he had changed all that. In his *Claudius*
(1703) he made the first barbarous attempt at a
mixture of Italian and German languages. It was
for him a pure fanfare of virtuosity, and he wished
to show, as he explained in his Preface, that he was
capable of beating the Italians on their own ground.
He took no account of the detriment to German
Opera. Handel, following his example, mixes, in his
first operas, the airs with Italian words with those
set to German words.[4] Since that time he no
longer wrote Italian operas ; and after that, his
musical theatre was without foundation and without
public. The sanction of this error resulted in Germany's neglect of Keiser's operas and even of those
of Handel, despite the genius of both composers.

.   .   .   .   .   .

[1] Such as the *Song of the Imprisoned Croesus*, which calls to
mind certain airs in *The Messiah*.
[2] I need only cite one example : it is the air of Octavia with
two soft flutes, " Wallet nicht zu laut," one of the most poetic
pages of Keiser, which Handel reproduced several times in his
works, and even in his *Acis and Galatea*, 1720.
[3] Postel, who used seven languages in the Prologues of his
Libretti, was opposed to this mixture in poetical works, " for
that which ornaments learning," he says, " disfigures poetry."
[4] Certain German operas mix High German, Low German,
French and Italian.

Handel arrived at Hamburg during the summer of 1703. One can imagine him there at that time of life as in the portrait painted by Thornhill, which is in the Fitzwilliam Museum at Cambridge : a long face, calm, but a little coarse, large and serious eyes, large and straight nose, ample forehead, vigorous mouth, with thick lips, cheeks and chin already full, very straight head without wig, and covered with a biretta after the manner of Wagner. " He was rich in power, and strong in will," says Mattheson, who, by the way, was the first acquaintance he made in Hamburg. Mattheson, who was then twenty-two,[1] four years older than Handel, came from a rich Hamburg family, and possessed vast knowledge. He spoke English, Italian, French, was trained for the law, well grounded in music, could play nearly all the instruments, and wrote operas, of which he was the poet, the composer, and the actor all in one. Above all he was a master theorist, and the most energetic critic of German music. With an immense *amour-propre* and many passionate dislikes, he had a robust spirit, very sound, and very honest, a sort of Boileau or of Lessing in music half a century before *la Dramaturgie*. On the one side he combated scholastic routine and abstract science in the name of nature, and laid down the rule that " music is that which sounds well " (" Musik, müsse schön klingen ").[2] He played his

---

[1] He was born at Hamburg in 1681, and died there in 1764. See L. Meinardus : *J. Mattheson und seine Verdienste um die deutsche Tonkunst,* 1870 ; and Heinrich Schmidt : *J. Mattheson, ein Förderer der deutschen Tonkunst,* 1897, Leipzig.

[2] He violently attacked in the *Volkommene Kapellmeister*

part in the banishment of the obsolete theories (solmisation, ecclesiastical modes) and the definition of our modern system.[1] On the other hand, he was the champion of German art and German spirit. From Lessing he derived his patriotism, his rough independence, his impetuosity, which seemed to possess a violence almost brutal. All his books cry " Fuori Barbari."[2] One of his works was entitled *The Musical Patriot (Der Musikalische Patriot,* 1728).

In 1722 he founded the first German musical journal, *Critica Musica,*[3] and all his life he waged

---

(1739) the " Pythagoreans " of whom the chief was Lor. Christoph Mizler, of Leipzig, who attempted to work out music on the lines of mathematics and logic. With the " Aristoxenians " (harmonists) he wished to rescue music from an iron vice, from the hands of the skeleton of a dead science, and from scholasticism. The ear was his law. " Let your art be encompassed where the ear alone reigns : that should suffice. Where nature and experience leads you, all is well. Do it, play it, sing it ; for wrong doing, avoid it, efface it " (*Das forschende Orchestre*). Against the scholastic, he opposed the fecund and living harmonic science (*Harmonische Wissenschaft*) ; he demanded that the latter should be taught in the universities, and offered to bequeath a large sum to found a Chair for a musical lectureship in the college of his native city.

[1] Especially in *Das neueröffnete Orchestre* (1713), *Das beschützte Orchestre* (1717), *Das forschende Orchestre* (1721). We might say that the most fruitful of his theoretical writings is *Der Vollkommene Kapellmeister* (1739), which might even to-day serve as the basis of a work on musical æsthetics, and that it was the work which produced a good part of our musicology.

[2] He warns German musicians against going to Italy, whence they return like so many birds plucked of their feathers, with their great weaknesses hidden, and an intolerable presumption. He reproached Germany with not helping her national musicians, who were languishing and becoming extinct (*Volk. Kapellm.* and *Critica Musica*).

[3] Twenty-four monthly books which appeared with interruptions from May, 1722, to 1725, Hamburg. There were musical polemics, correspondence, interviews with musicians, analyses of their books and works, a shoal of letters on the last opera, on

a vigorous war for good sense, real musical intelligence, music which speaks to the heart and not to the ear, moving and strengthening the soul of the intelligent man with beautiful thoughts and melodies.[1] He saw in music a religious idea.[2] By his wide culture, his knowledge of the artistic theories of the past, his familiarity with all the important French and Italian works, his relationships with the principal German masters, with Keiser, Handel, J. S. Bach, by his rich practical experience, his acute critical sense, his ardent patriotism, his virile and flowing language, he was well fitted to be the great musical educator of Germany, and he accomplished his task well. In the dispersion of German artists which took place then, in addition to the many vicissitudes of their work, there was chiefly lacking a support of political solidarity which could cause music to rise above the fluctuations of the tastes of little towns and the small coteries. Mattheson was then for half a century the sole tribune of German music, the intellect where thoughts concentrated from all

the last concert, on the life of a musician, on a new clavier, on a singer, etc. One finds pre-eminently very solid musical critiques, perhaps the oldest which exist. The minute analysis of Handel's *Passion according to St. John* was still celebrated when the work itself was forgotten. " It is perhaps," said Marpurg in 1760, " the first good critique which was written on choral music " since it sprang into being.

[1] *Critica Musica.*

[2] " When I think as a tone-poet (Tondichter)," he says, " I think of something higher than a great figure. . . . Formerly musicians were poets and prophets." In another place he writes, " It is the property of music to be above all sciences a school of virtue, *eine Zuchtlehre* " (*Vollk. Kapellm.*).

quarters, and from him radiated an influence over
all the country in return. It was thus that he
preserved the ideas of Keiser, which apart from
him would have fallen into oblivion without leaving
any traces of their existence. It was these traces
that he rescued out of the *débâcle* and preserved for
us—a multitude of imperishable souvenirs for the
musical history of the eighteenth century—which
Mattheson gathered together and published in his
monumental *Ehrenpforte*.[1] He acted powerfully on
his times. His books laid down the law for the
Kapellmeisters, the Cantors, the organists, and the
teachers.

His criticisms, his advice on style in singing, on
gesture in acting, were no less efficacious. He
possessed the real " theatre " feeling. He expected
life in the stage action, attaching considerable
importance to the pantomime " which is a silent
music."[2] He waged war against the impossible
action and the want of intelligence amongst the
German singers and choralists, and he desired that
the composer should think always in writing of the
action of the player. " The knowledge of facial
expression by the actors on the stage," says he,
" can often be a source of good musical ideas."[3]
This is indeed the language of a true man of the

---

[1] *Grundlagen einer Ehrenpforte, worin der tüchtigsten Kapellmeister, Komponisten, Musikgelehrten, Tonkünstler, etc. Leben,
Werke, Verdienste, etc., erscheinen sollen,* 1740.

[2] *Vollkommene Kapellmeister,* 1739—he devoted a very important study, which he called the *Hypokritik* (Pantomime) to it,
in this work.

[3] *Ibid.*

theatre.[1] For the rest, Mattheson was too good a musician to serve music in words. He sought to unite them by safeguarding the independence of both, but ended by giving the preference to the soul over the body, the melody over the words. The words he wrote are the body of the discourses ; the thoughts are the soul ; the melody is the sun shining on the soul, the marvellous atmosphere which envelops it all. We have said enough to give some idea of this great critic, intelligent and intrepid, who, with many faults, has yet many virtues. One will see how important it was to the young Handel to meet such a guide, even though they were both too original and too self-sufficient for the association to last long.

.   .   .   .   .

Mattheson did Handel the honours of Hamburg. He introduced him at the Opera, and the concerts, and it was through him that Handel entered for the first time into negotiations with England, which was to become his second country.[2] They helped

[1] In theory rather than in practice : for his operas are mediocre. Besides, he soon lost his taste for the theatre, his religious scruples being too strong for him. He wished at first to purify the Opera, to make the theatre something serious and sacred, which should act on the masses in an instructive and elevating manner (*Musikalischer Patriot*, 1728). Then he saw that his conception of a moral and edifying opera had no chance of being realised. Finally he lost his interest, and even rejoiced in 1750 over the final ruin which overtook the Hamburg Opera.

[2] Mattheson, who spoke perfect English, and who became a little later the secretary to the English Legation, then resident in the interim, presented Handel to the English Ambassador, John Wich, who entrusted them both with the instruction of his son.

one another mutually. Handel had already an
exceptional power on the organ, and in fugue and
counterpoint ; above all, in improvisation. He
shared his knowledge with Mattheson, who in return
helped him to perfect his melodic style. Mattheson
believed him to be a very feeble melodist. He wrote
his melodies at that time, " Oh, long, long, long "
(*sehr lange lange Arien*), and cantatas without end,
which had neither ability nor good taste, but
perfect harmony.[1]   It is very remarkable that
melody was not a natural gift with Handel, for he
now appears to us as a melodic genius. It is not
necessary to believe that the simple, beautiful
melodies rushed forth without effort from his brain.
The melodies of Beethoven, which seem the most
spontaneous, cost him years of thoughtful work
during which he brooded continually over them, and
so Handel also only came to his full power of
melodic expression after years of severe discipline,
where he learnt as an apprentice-sculptor to model
beautiful forms, and to leave them neither complex
nor unfinished.

Handel and Mattheson spent several months in
intimate friendship.[2]   Handel joined Mattheson at
table for meals, and in July and August, 1703, they
made a journey together to Lubeck to hear the

---

[1] *Ehrenpforte.*—Telemann, a co-disciple of Handel, says also
that both Handel and he worked continually at melody.

[2] With a kind of protective touch, however, on the part of
Mattheson. During the first months Handel would never have
dreamt of offending him. The style of his letters to Mattheson
in March, 1704, was extremely respectful. In fact Mattheson
was then in advance of him, and his superior in social
position.

renowned organist, Dietrich Buxtehude.[1] Buxtehude had thoughts of retiring, and was looking for a successor. The two young men were greatly affected by his talent, but they did not care to succeed him in the post, for it was necessary to wed his daughter[2] to have his organ, and, said Mattheson, " neither of them wanted her."—Two years later they would have met on the road to Lubeck a young musician also going, like them, to pay Buxtehude a visit, not like them, however, in a carriage, but more humbly on foot : J. S. Bach.[3] Nothing makes us realise the importance of Buxtehude in German musie better than this magnet-like attraction which he exercised over the German musicians of the eighteenth century. Pirro has remarked at some length his influence on the organ style of J. S. Bach. I consider that it was no less marked, though quite different, on the oratorio style of Handel.[4]

[1] See in the *Ehrenpforte* the story of this journey, and the frolics which happened on the way to the two joyful companions.
Buxtehude was a Dane, born at Elsinore in 1637. He settled at Lubeck, where he remained as the organist of St. Mary's Church, from the age of thirty years until his death in 1707.
[2] It was the custom that the organ of a church should be given with the daughter, or the widow of the organist. Buxtehude himself, in succeeding Tunder, had married his daughter.
[3] J. S. Bach went to Lubeck in October, 1705, and instead of staying a month, as arranged, he spent four months there ; an irregularity which cost him his position at Celle.
[4] The organ works of Buxtehude have been republished by Spitta and Max Seiffert, in 2 volumes by Breitkopf (see the short, but pithy, study of Pirro in his little book on *L'Orgue de J. S. Bach*, Paris, 1895, and Max Seiffert : *Buxtehude, Handel, Bach*, in the Peter's Annual, 1902). A selection (too restricted) of the cantatas has been published in a volume of the *Denkmäler deutscher Tonkunst*. Pirro is preparing a longer work on Buxtehude.

Buxtehude gave at St. Mary's Church, Lubeck, his celebrated *Abendmusiken* (evening concerts), which took place on Sundays from St. Martin's Day to Christmas,[1] by the request of the Merchants' Guilds at Lubeck, which occupied themselves keenly with music.[2] His cantatas, of which the number is considerable,[3] were all composed for these occasions. Writing for a concert public, and not for a religious service, he felt the need of making his music of a kind which would appeal to everyone. Handel later on found himself in similar circumstances, and the same need led them both to a similar technique. Buxtehude avoided in his music the ornate and clustering polyphony which was really his *métier*.[4] He sought nothing but clear, pleasing, and striking designs, and even aimed at descriptive music. He willingly sacrificed himself, by intensifying his expression, and what he lost in abundance he gained in power. The homophonic character of his writing, the neatness of his beautiful melodic designs of a popular clarity,[5] the insistence of the rhythms and the repetition of phrases which sink down into the heart in so obsessive a manner,

[1] Particularly during 1693.

[2] The part played by these free cities, Hamburg, Lubeck, the abodes of intelligent and adventurous merchants, in the history of German music, should be specially noticed. The part is analogous to that played by Venice and Florence in Italian painting and music.

[3] There are about 150 manuscripts in the libraries of Lubeck, Upsala, Berlin, Wolfenbüttel, and Brussels.

[4] His organ music bears witness to his mastery in this style.

[5] See the penetrating intimacy, the suave melody, of the cantata *Alles was ihr tut mit Worten oder Werken*, and the tragic grandeur with such simple means of the magnificent cantata *Gott hilf mir*.

are all essentially Handelian traits. No less is the magnificent triumph of the ensembles, his manner of painting in bold masses of light and shade.[1] It is to a very high degree, as with the art of Handel, music for everyone.

But much time passed before Handel profited by the examples of Buxtehude. On his return from Lubeck he seems to have forgotten them. It was not so, however, for nothing was ever lost on him.

At the end of August, 1703, Handel entered the Hamburg orchestra as a second violinist. He loved to amuse himself amongst his kind, and he often made himself appear more ignorant than he was. " He behaved," said Mattheson, " as if he did not even know how to count five, for he was a ' dry stick.' "[2] That year at Hamburg, Keiser's *Claudius* was given at the Opera, and many of the phrases registered themselves in Handel's marvellous memory.[3]

When the season was finished, Mattheson made a journey to Holland, and Handel profited by the absence of his young adviser to assert his own individuality. He had made the acquaintance of the poet Postel, who, old, ill, and troubled by

[1] We find on page 167 of the *Denkmäler* volume, a *Hallelujah* by Buxtehude for 2 clarini (trumpets), 2 violins, 2 violas, violoncello, organ, and 5 vocal parts, which is pure Handel, and very beautiful.

[2] Mattheson adds : " I know with certainty that if he reads these pages, he will laugh up his sleeve, but outwardly he laughs little."

[3] Amongst others, the subject from an air in minuet form, which he repeated exactly in the minuet of his overture to *Samson*.

religious scruples, had given up the writing of opera
libretti, and no longer wished to compose anything
but sacred works.   Postel furnished Handel with
the text for a *Passion according to Saint John*, which
Handel set to music, and performed during Holy
Week in 1704.[1] Mattheson, piqued at the *volte face*
which had happened in his relationship with Handel,
criticised the music severely, but not unjustly.[2]
Despite the intense feeling of certain pages, and the
fine dramatic nature of the choruses, the work was
uneven, and occasionally lacked good taste.

From this moment the friendship between Handel
and Mattheson was finished.   Handel became
conscious of his own genius, and could no longer
stand the protectorship of Mattheson.   Other
occurrences aggravated the misunderstanding, which
ended in a quarrel, which narrowly escaped a fatal
issue.[3] Following the altercation at the Opera on

[1] In the same week, Keiser and the poet Hunold gave another
Passion, *The Bleeding and Dying Jesus*, which made a scandal :
for he had treated the subject in the manner of an opera, suppressing the chorales, the chief songs, and the person of the
evangelist and his story.   Handel and Postel more prudently
only suppressed the songs, but reserved the text of the evangelist.
[2] This criticism, certainly written in 1704, was repeated by
Mattheson in his musical journal, *Critica Musica*, in 1725, and
even twenty years later on, in his *Wollkommene Kapellmeister*,
in 1740.
[3] The two young men had charge of the education of the
English Ambassador's son, Mattheson in the position of chief
tutor, Handel as music master.   Mattheson took advantage of
the situation to inflict on Handel a humiliating rebuke.   Handel
revenged himself by ridiculing Mattheson, whose *Cleopatra* was
being given at the Opera.   Mattheson conducted the orchestra
from the clavier, and took the *rôle* of Antony as well.   When he
played the part he left the clavier to Handel, but after Antony
had died, an hour before the end of the play, Mattheson returned
in theatrical costume to the clavier, so as not to miss the final

December 5, 1704, they fought a duel in the
market-place at Hamburg, and Handel only
escaped being killed by a stroke of luck: for
Mattheson's sword snapped on a large metal button
on Handel's coat, after which they embraced, and
the two companions, reconciled by Keiser, took
part together in the rehearsals of *Almira*, the first
opera of Handel.[1] The first representation took
place on January 8, 1705, and the work was a
brilliant success. A second opera of Handel, *Nero*[2]
was played on February 25 following, but it had
not quite the success of *Almira*. Handel himself occupied the placards of the opera during
the whole of the winter season. It was a fine
début. Too fine indeed, and Keiser became jealous
of him. The Hamburg Opera, however, was
gradually waning. Keiser gaily led it to its ruin.

ovations. Handel, who had submitted to this little comedy for
the first two representations, refused on the third to give his
chair to Mattheson. In the end they came to fisticuffs. The
story is told in a rather confusing manner by Mattheson in his
Ehrenpforte, and by Mainwaring, who sided with Handel.

[1] *Der in Krohnen erlangte Glücks-Wechsel, oder Almira
Konigen von Castilien* (The Adventures of the Fortune of the
Kings, or Almira, Queen of Castile). The libretti was drawn
from a comedy by Lope de Vega by a certain Feustking, whose
scandalous life Chrysander has recorded, and also the battle of
the ribald pamphlets with Barthold Feind on the subject of
this piece. Keiser ought to have written the music of *Almira*,
but, being too occupied with his business and his amusements,
he handed the book over to Handel.

Once for all I will say here that the exigences of this book
will not allow of any analysis of Handel's operas. I hope to
give detailed analyses of them in another book on Handel and
his times (*Musiciens d'autrefois*, Second Series).

[2] *Die durch Blut und Mord erlangte Liebe, oder Nero* (Love
obtained by blood and crime, or Nero), poem by Feustking.
Mattheson played the part of Nero. The musical score is lost.

D

He led the life of a gay libertine, and all the artists around him rivalled him in his follies. Alone Handel held aloof from the follies, working hard, and spending only what was barely necessary.[1] After the success of these two operas he resigned his post as second violin and clavecinist to the orchestra, but continued to give lessons, and his reputation as a composer kept pace with that of his teaching. Keiser was uneasy. Handel's increasing reputation aroused his *amour-propre*. Nothing was more stupid, however, than his jealousy. He was Director of the Opera, and it was in his interest to give those pieces which were written by popular composers, and to maintain relationships with successful composers, but jealousy knows no reason. He reset *Almira* and *Nero* to music in order to put Handel out of joint,[2] and as he had not the opportunity of publishing his opera *in toto* he hastily printed the most taking solos from each.[3] But, however quickly he went, his downfall followed faster. Before the volume of his opera airs appeared

[1] In 1703 Handel returned his mother the allowance which she made him, and added thereto certain presents for Christmas. In 1704, 1705 and 1706 he saved two hundred ducats for his travels in Italy.

[2] The new *Nero* was played under the title of *Die Romische Unruhe, oder die edelmüthige Octavia* (The troubles of Rome, or the magnanimous Octavia). The score has been republished in the supplements to the Complete Handel Edition by Max Seiffert with Breitkopf. *Almira* took the title : *Der Durchlanchtige Secretarius, oder Almira, Königen in Castilien* (His Excellency the Secretary, or Almira, Queen of Castile).

Besides these two works, Keiser wrote in two years, seven operas, the finest he had done, an evident proof of his genius, which, however, lacked the character and dignity worthy of it.

[3] Under the title *Componimenti Musicali*, 1706, Hamburg.

he had to fly. This was in the end of 1706.[1] Handel
and he were destined never to meet again.

.   .   .   .   .   .

Keiser having brought disaster to the Hamburg
Opera, there was nothing left to keep Handel in
that city. The direction of the theatre had fallen
into the hands of a Philistine, who, to make money,
played musical farces. He certainly commissioned
Handel for the opera *Florindo und Daphne*, but he
mutilated the work on its presentation " for fear,"
so he said in the Preface of the libretto, " that the
music might tire the hearers "; and lest the public
should find the work too serious, he intersected it
with a farce in low German, *Die lustige Hochzeit*
(The Joyous Wedding). One can well understand
that Handel was little interested in his piece so
disfigured, and that he did not himself attend the
production, but quitted Hamburg. It was about
the autumn of 1706 that he made the journey to
Italy.[2] It was not, however, that Italy particularly attracted him. Strange to say—it is not
unique in the history of art—this man, who was

[1] For the space of two years no one knew what had become
of him, for he had taken care to elude the restraint of his creditors.
At the beginning of 1709 he quietly reappeared in Hamburg,
took up again his post and his glory, without anyone dreaming
of reproaching him, but then Handel was no longer at Hamburg.

[2] Besides the operas, and his *Passion*, Handel wrote at
Hamburg a large number of cantatas, songs, and clavier works.
Mainwaring assures us that he had two cases full of them.
Mattheson doubts the truth of this statement, but the ignorance
which he shows on this subject only goes to prove his growing
estrangement from Handel, for we have since found both in his
clavier book, etc. (Volume XLVIII of the complete works), and
in the Sonatas (Volume XXVII) a number of compositions which
certainly date from the Hamburg period 1705 or 1706.

later on to be caught by the fascination of Italy, and secure an European musical triumph in the beautiful Italian style, had then a very strong repugnance for the foreign art. When *Almira* was being given, he made the acquaintance of the Italian prince, Giovanni Gastone dei Medici, brother of the Grand Duke of Tuscany.[1] He was astonished that Handel interested himself so little in the Italian musicians, and bought him a collection of their best works, offering to take him to Florence to hear them performed. But Handel refused, saying that he could find nothing in these works which deserved the Prince's eulogies, and that angels would be necessary to sing them in order to make such mediocre things sound even agreeable.[2] This disdain of Italy was not peculiar to Handel. It characterised his generation, and above all, the cult of German musicians who lived at Hamburg. Before then, and later on, the fascination of Italy took hold of Germany. Even Hasler, Schütz, Hasse, Gluck, and Mozart made long and earnest pilgrimages to that country, but on the other hand J. S. Bach, Keiser, Mattheson, and Telemann never went there. The Hamburg musicians truly wished to assimilate the Italian art, but they never wished to place themselves under the thraldom of the

---

[1] He was the last of the Medici. He came to the title in 1723, but after several years of brilliant rule he retired into solitude, sick in body and in spirit (see Reumont : *Toscana*, and Robiony : *Gli Ultimi dei Medici*).

[2] Later on Handel said after he had been to Italy that he never had imagined that Italian music, which appears so ordinary and empty on paper, could make such a good effect in the theatre itself.

Italian school. They had the laudable ambition of creating a German style independent of foreign influences. Handel shared these great hopes, sustained for a time by the theatre at Hamburg, but the sudden collapse of this theatre made him see little ground on which to build up the taste of the musical public in Germany, and against his own inclinations, he turned his eyes towards that habitual refuge of German artists : Italy, which the older ones so affected to disdain, that country where music expanded itself in the sun, where it was not cheated out of its right of existence as with the Hamburg Pietists. It flourished in all the Italian cities, and in all classes of Italian society with the transports of love. And all around it was an efflorescence of the other arts, a superior civilization, a life smiling and radiant, of which Handel had some foretaste in his dealings with the Italian nobles who passed through Hamburg.

He departed. His leaving was so brusque that his friends knew nothing of it. He did not even say good-bye to Mattheson.

The period at which he arrived in Italy was not the most fortunate. The war for the Spanish Succession was in full swing, and Handel met at Venice, in the winter of 1706, Prince Eugène and his staff-major, who were resting after their victorious campaign in Lombardy. He did not stay there, but went right on to Florence, where he remained till the end of the year.[1]

[1] Mr. R. A. Streatfeild believes that he even stayed in Florence until October, 1706, for the Prince Gastone dei Medici,

Doubtless he bore these offers of protection in mind which the Prince Gastone dei Medici had made him. Was such protection as useful to Handel as he had hoped ? One may be allowed to doubt it. In truth the son of the Grand Duke of Tuscany, Ferdinand, was a musician. He played the clavier well ;[1] he had caused an opera house to be built in his villa at Pratolino ; he chose the *libretti*, advised the composers, corresponded with Alessandro Scarlatti, but he had never a very reliable taste. He found Scarlatti's style too learned. He begged him to write some easier music, and, as far as possible, lighter.[2] He himself did not continue the fastidiousness of the Medici, his ancestors. He somewhat stinted his outlay on music. He decided not to appoint Scarlatti his chapel-master, and when this great artist asked for money at a period of embarrassment he responded " that he would pray for him."[3] One can scarcely believe that he was less economical in his dealings with Handel, who had less reputation than Scarlatti. He seems to have paid little attention to him during his first visit. The Prince himself seemed out of his element in this new world. It was necessary for him to

who ought to have presented him to the Grand Duke, left Florence in November, 1706. He also places in this first sojourn in Florence the production of Handel's *Roderigo*, of which all precise records in the archives of the Medicis and the papers of the time are lost. I am more inclined to follow the traditional opinion that *Roderigo* dates from Handel's second stay in Florence, when he commenced to work in the Italian language and style.

[1] Bartolommeo Christofori, inventor of the pianoforte, made several very interesting instruments for him.

[2] April 2, 1706.

[3] April 23, 1707. See Edward Dent : *Alessandro Scarlatti*.

catch up with his times. Handel certainly wrote some cantatas, only one of which, *Lucretia*, with a dramatic character, was very popular in Italy and in Germany later on.[1] Its style was nearly completely German.

From Florence he went to Rome for the Easter festivals in April, 1707. Even there the moment was not very favourable for him. The Grand Opera House, the *Tor di Nona*, had been destroyed as immoral by an edict of Pope Innocent XII ten years before. Since 1700, things had been a little easier for the musicians, but in 1703 a terrible earthquake had desolated the country, and reawakened religious qualms.[2] Even in 1709, during the whole of Handel's sojourn in Italy, there was not a single representation of Opera at Rome. On the other hand, religious music and chamber music were enjoying a great vogue. Handel, during the first months, listened and studied the religious music at Rome, and tried his hand on similar works. From this period dated his Latin Psalms.[3] Thanks to the

---

[1] Volume LI of the Complete Works. It was pretended at the time that this *Lucretia* was written by one Lucretia, a singer at the court of Tuscany, who showed Handel for the first time the great beauty of the Italian song—and of the Italians.

[2] The whole of Europe in the commencement of the eighteenth century had passed through a vogue of Pietism. Historians have scarcely paid sufficient attention to local influences. It was thus that they attributed the reawakening of the religious spirit in France entirely to the influence of Louis XIV. Analogous phenomena were produced in Italy, in Germany, and in England, at the same time. There were great moral forces awakening, which, one cannot exactly say why, suddenly broke out over the whole of the civilized world like a stroke of fever.

[3] A *Dixit Dominus* is dated April 4, 1707 ; a *Laudate Pueri*, July 8, 1707.

letters of recommendation he had from the Medici,
he had also been introduced into the Roman *salons*.
He became famous there, more on account of his
virtuoso powers on the keyboard than of those of
composer. He remained at Rome until the autumn
of 1707.[1] Doubtless, he returned to Florence in the
month of October, and it appears that he then produced *Roderigo* for the first time. Handel had then
been nearly a year in Italy. He set about writing
an opera in Italian. His boldness was justified.
Roderigo was successful. Handel gained through it
the favour of the Grand Duke, and the love of the
Prima Donna, Vittoria Tarquini.[2] Fortified by his
first victory he went on to try his luck at Venice.

Venice was then the musical metropolis of Italy.
It was in a way the real kingdom of Opera. The
first public opera house had been already open
there for half a century, and after it, fifteen other
opera houses had sprung into being. During the
Carnival no less than seven opera houses were open
each evening there. Every night also a musical
union was held at the Academy of Music, and
occasionally twice or even three times in one
evening. Every day in the churches, musical

[1] A letter from Annibale Merlini to Ferdinando dei Medici,
recently published by Mr. Streatfeild, says that on September
24, 1707, the famous Saxon (*Il Sassone famoso*), as Handel was
already called, was still enchanting hearers in the musical
evenings at Rome.

[2] Both Mr. Andimolo, in an article in the *Nuova Antologia*,
July 16, 1889, and Mr. Streatfeild, have established the true
name of the chief singer in *Roderigo*. Thus the romantic story
believed ever since Chrysander of Handel's love for the famous
Vittoria Tesi has been destroyed. She was only seven years old
in 1707, and did not come out until 1716.

solemnities and concerts, which lasted for many
hours, with several orchestras, many organs, and
numerous full and echo choirs,[1] and on Saturday
and Sunday the famous Vespers of the Hospitals,
those conservatoires for women where they taught
music to orphans and foundlings, or, more frequently,
to the girls who had fine voices. They gave
orchestral and vocal concerts, over which all Venice
raved. Venice, indeed, was bathed in music, the
entire life was threaded with it. Life was a perpetual round of pleasure.

When Handel arrived, the greatest of the Italian
musicians, Alessandro Scarlatti, was about to
produce at St. John Chrysostom's Theatre his
chief work, *Mitridate Eupatore*, one of the rare
Italian operas of which the dramatic beauty is on
a par with the musical value. Was Alessandro
Scarlatti still in Venice when Handel met him ?
We do not know, but in any case he encountered
him at Rome some months later, and it appears
that at that time Handel was tied by bonds of
friendship to the son of Alessandro,—Domenico.[2]
He also made many other encounters in Venice,
which were destined to change his life. The Prince

[1] Occasionally in St. Mark's there were six orchestras, two large
ones in the galleries with the two grand organs, four smaller ones
distributed in pairs in the lower galleries, each with two small
organs.

[2] Mainwaring relates that Handel arrived *incognito* at Venice,
and that he was discovered in a masquerade where he was playing
the clavier. Domenico Scarlatti cried out that it must either be
the celebrated Saxon, or the devil. This story, which shows that
Handel was celebrated already as a virtuoso, accords very well
with his taste for mystifying people, a marked trait in his character.

of Hanover, Ernest Augustus, and the Duke of Manchester, the English Ambassador Extraordinary at Venice, were both passionate music-lovers, and interested themselves in Handel. The first invitations which Handel received to go to Hanover, and to London, dated doubtless from that time.

But if the visit to Venice was not fruitless to the future of Handel, it brought him very little at the time. Handel could produce nothing at any of the seven opera houses.[1] He was much happier at Rome, where he returned at the beginning of March, 1708.[2] The renown of his *Roderigo* had preceded him. All the Italian merchants strove to receive him with honour. He was the guest of the Marquis Ruspoli, whose gardens on the Esquilino formed the bond of reunion for the Academy of the Arcadians.[3] Handel found himself agreeably placed amongst the most illustrious men which Italy boasted in literature, the arts, and in the aristocracy. Arcadia, which united the nobility and the artists,[4] in a spiritual brotherhood, counted amongst its members,

[1] This appears thoroughly established by recent researches, and contradicts the statement of Chrysander that Handel's *Agrippina* had been played at the commencement of 1708 at Venice. All the documents of that time agree in placing the first production of *Agrippina* at the end of 1709 or at the beginning of 1710.

[2] An autograph cantata by Handel, which is found in London, was dated Rome, March 3, 1708.

[3] This Academy was founded at Rome in 1690 for the production and exposition of popular poetry and rhetoric.

[4] Amongst the "shepherds" of Arcadia were counted four Popes (Clement XI, Innocent XIII, Clement XII, Benoit XIII), nearly all the sacred colleges, the Princes of Bavaria, Poland, Portugal; the Queen of Poland, the Grand Duchess of Tuscany, and a crowd of great lords and ladies.

Alessandro Scarlatti, Archangelo Corelli, Bernardo Pasquini, and Benedetto Marcello.[1] A similar *élite* society was found at the *soirées* of the Cardinal Ottoboni.[2] Every Monday, in the palace of Ottoboni, as at the meetings of the Arcadia, concerts and poetical recitations were given. The Cardinal Prince, Superintendent of the Pontifical chapel, had in his service the finest orchestra in Italy,[3] and the singers of the Sistine Chapel. At the Arcadia there was also to be heard a numerous orchestra, under the direction of Corelli, of Pasquini, or of Scarlatti. Musical and poetical improvisation was also given there. It was that which provoked the artistic jousts between poets and musicians.[4] It was for the concerts at the palace of Ottoboni that Handel

[1] Scarlatti under the name of Terpandro ; Corelli under that of Archimelo ; Pasquini as Protico ; Marcello as Dryanti. Handel was not inscribed on the Arcadia list because he was not yet of the regulation age, twenty-four years.

[2] Cardinal Ottoboni was a Venetian, and nephew of the Pope Alexander VIII. A good priest, very benevolent, and ostentatious art patron whose prodigalities were celebrated even in England, where Dryden eulogised them in 1691 in the Prologue of Purcell's *King Arthur*. He was a great *dilettante*, and even wrote an opera himself, *Il Columbo, overo l'India scoperta*, 1691. Alessandro Scarlatti set to music his libretto of *Statira*, and composed for him his *Rosaura*, and his *Christmas Oratorio*. He was particularly intimate with Corelli, who lived with him.

[3] Corelli took the first violin, and Francischiello, the violoncello.

[4] At one meeting of the Arcadia in April, 1706, Alessandro Scarlatti seated himself at the keyboard, whilst the poet Zappi improvised a poem. Hardly had Zappi finished reciting the last verse than Scarlatti improvised music on the verses—similarly at Ottoboni's house Handel improvised many secular cantatas whilst the Cardinal Panfili improvised the verses. It is related that one of these poems constituted a Dithyrambic eulogy, and that Handel, unperturbed, amused himself by setting it to music, and doubtless singing it.

wrote his two Roman oratorios, *The Resurrection* and *The Triumph of Time and Truth*,[1] which were really but disguised operas. One finds traces of the Arcadia *coterie* in the compositions which are perhaps the most characteristic of this period in the life of Handel: the Italian cantatas,[2] of which the reputation spread itself very wide, for J. S. Bach made a copy of one of them before 1715.[3] Handel passed three or four months at Rome. He was friendly with Corelli, and with the two Scarlattis, especially with the son, Domenico, who made many trials of virtuosity with him.[4] Perhaps he also played with Bernardo Pasquini, whom he doubtless heard more than once on his organ at Great St. Mary's. He was interested in the life of the Vatican, and they tried to convert him to Catholicism, but he refused. Such was the friendly tolerance which prevailed then at the Court of Rome that, notwithstanding the war between the Pope and Emperor, this refusal did not alter the friendly relationships between the young German Lutheran

[1] The manuscript of *The Resurrection* bears this superscription: April 11, 1708, *La Festa de Pasque dal Marche Ruspoli* (The Easter Festival at the Marquis Ruspoli's).

[2] They occupy four volumes in the great Breitkopf edition— two volumes of cantatas, of solo cantatas, with single bass for clavier, and two volumes of cantatas *Con stromenti*, of which certain are serenatas for two or three parts.

[3] The *Armida abbandonata*. The copy, very carefully penned in the writing of Bach, is now lodged in the house of Breitkopf.

[4] It is related that at one of the Ottoboni evenings there was a contest on the clavier and on the organ between Domenico Scarlatti and Handel. The result was undecided on the clavier, but for the organ Scarlatti himself was the first to declare Handel the victor. After that, whenever Scarlatti spoke of him he always made the sign of the Cross.

and the Cardinals, his patrons. He became so
attached to Rome, that it was difficult for him to
leave it until the war which approached the city
obliged him to take his way in the month of May
or June, 1708, to Naples. One of the Italian
cantatas entitled *Partenza* shows his grief at leaving
the lovely banks, the dear walls, and the beautiful
waters of the Tiber.

Soon after his arrival at Naples, Alessandro
Scarlatti returned to settle there after seven years
of absence.[1]

Thanks to this friendship, and his membership
of the Arcadia, Handel was received into the best
circles of Neapolitan society. He remained at
Naples for nearly a year, from June, 1708, to the
spring of 1709, enjoying princely hospitality, " which
placed at his disposal," says Mainwaring, " a palace,
a well-supplied table, and a coach." If the softness
of the Italian life enervated him, he appears to have
wasted no time. Not only did he assimilate the
style of his friend Corelli—he conceived in Italy a
passionate love of pictures[2]—but he attempted with
a carefully cultivated dilettantism the most diverse
styles, with which the cosmopolitan society of
Naples amused its careless curiosity. Spanish and

---

[1] Scarlatti was attached to the Royal Chapel of Naples as
principal Organist in December, 1708. Then he was reinstated
in this post in January, 1709, and in the course of the same year
he was nominated master of the Conservatoire of *Poveri di Gesù
Cristo*.

[2] All his life one of his chief hobbies—as with Corelli and
Hasse—was to visit picture galleries. It is necessary to note
this visual intelligence with the great German and Italian
musicians of this period, since one does not find it with those
of the end of the eighteenth century.

French influence fought for the honours of this city.
Handel, as indifferent as Scarlatti to the victory of
either of these parties, tried to write in the style of
both.[1] He interested himself also in the Italian
popular songs and noted down the rustic melodies
of the Calabrian *Pifferari*.[2] For the Arcadians of
Naples he wrote his beautiful serenata, *Acis and
Galatea*.[3] Finally he had the good fortune to please
the Viceroy of Naples—the Cardinal Grimani. He
was a Venetian and his family owned the theatre
of San Grisostomo at Venice. Grimani wrote for
Handel the libretto of the opera *Agrippina*, of which
Handel probably composed part of the music at
Naples. A similar collaboration assured it of being
produced at Venice without trouble.

He left Naples in the springtime, and returned to
Rome, where he met, at the Palace of the Cardinal
Ottoboni, Bishop Agostino Steffani, who by a
curious combination of attributes was at the same
time Kapellmeister at the Court of Hanover, and
charged with secret missions by different German

[1] One of his cantatas is preserved, *Cantata spagnola a voce sola
a chitarra* (Spanish Cantata for solo voice and guitar, published
in the second volume of Italian cantatas *Con stromenti*), and
seven French songs in the style of Lully, with accompaniment of
Figured Bass for the clavier. One copy of these songs is found
in the Conservatoire Library, Paris (Fonds Schoelcher).

[2] One of them forms the inspiration for the Pastoral Symphony
of *The Messiah*. Handel also acquired in Italy his taste for the
Siciliano, which became the rage in Naples, and which he
used, after *Agrippina*, in nearly all his operas, and even in his
oratorios.

[3] The *Acis and Galatea* of 1708 has no relation to the one
of 1720, but in taking up the later work in 1732 Handel made a
rearrangement of his Italian serenade, and gave it in London,
mingling with it the English airs of his other *Acis*.

princes.[1] Steffani was one of the most finished musicians of his time. He established a firm friendship with Handel, possibly when travelling together to Venice, where Handel's *Agrippina* was played at the opening of the Carnival season, 1709–10, at the theatre of San Giovanni Grisostomo.[2] The success exceeded all anticipations. Mainwaring says that he took all his hearers by storm. There were great acclamations, and cries of *Viva il caro Sassone* and extravagances impossible to record. The grandeur of the style struck them all like thunder. The Italians had good reason to rejoice, for they found in Handel a most brilliant exponent, and *Agrippina* is the most melodious of his Italian operas. Venice then made and unmade reputations. The enthusiasm aroused by the representations at San Giovanni Grisostomo's spread itself out over the whole of musical Europe. Handel remained the whole of the winter at Venice. He seemed undecided as to what course to follow. It was quite

[1] Concerning Steffani, see page 51 and following. It seems quite compatible with this meeting with Handel at Rome in 1709 to relate the story made by Handel of a concert at Ottoboni's, where Steffani supplied the improvisation of one of the chief singers with a consummate art. Chrysander places this story at the time of the second Italian journey of Handel in 1729, but that is impossible, for Steffani died in February, 1728.

[2] That is to say on December 26, 1709. That is the date which the recent researches of Mr. Andimollo and Mr. Streatfeild have established in accordance with the indications of the contemporary histories of Handel by Mattheson, Marpurg, and Burney, of the date inscribed on the *libretto* itself. This contradicts the statement of Chrysander adopted on his authority by most of the musical writers of our own time, stating that *Agrippina* was played at Venice in the Carnival of 1708.

on the cards that he should pass through Paris.[1]
Handel had familiarised himself with the French
language.[2] He showed, as it happened, a singular
attraction for the most beautiful subjects of our
French tragedy.[3] With his prodigious adaptability,
and his Latin qualities, the clarity of his lines, his
eloquence, logic, and his passionate love for form,
he would have rejoiced exceedingly in assimilating
the tradition of our art, and taking it up with an
irresistible vigour.[4] But at Venice, whilst he was
still hesitating what to do, he encountered the

[1] There was so much probability of this that he tried his
hand on the French vocal style by writing seven French songs,
of which the manuscript was carefully revised by him, for the
sheets contain evidences of a close revision in pencil. How
changed things would have been there if he had really come and
settled in the interregnum between Lully and Rameau. He had
that quality which none of the French musicians possessed—a
superabundance of music, and he had not that which they had
got—lucid intelligence and a penetration into the true need of
the musical drama and its possibilities. (It was at that time
that Lecerf de la Vieville wrote his *Comparaison de la musique
française et de la musique italienne*, of which certain pages forestall
the musical creed of Gluck.) If Handel had come to France, I
am convinced that that reform would have been brought about
sixty years sooner, and with a wealth of music which Gluck
never possessed.

[2] It is the language which he used in his correspondence, even
with his own family, and his style, always very correct, had
the fine courtesy of the court of Louis XIV.

[3] *Esther, Athalie, Theodore, Vierge d'Martyre.*

[4] Even in 1734 Séré de Rieux wrote of Handel: " His
composition, infinitely clever and gracious, seems to approach
nearer to our taste than any other in Europe " (p. 29 of *Enfants
de Latone*, poems dedicated to the King). Handel particularly
pleased the French because his Italianism was always restrained
by reason, and French musicians loved to think that logic was
totally French.

" Son caractère fort, nouveau, brillant, égal,
    Du sens judicieux suit la constante trace,
    Et ne s'arme jamais d'une insolente audace."

Ibid. (pp. 102–3.)

Hanoverian nobles, amongst whom was the Baron
Kielmansegg, who invited him to follow them.
Steffani himself had offered him with a charming
grace his post as Kapellmeister at the Court of
Hanover. Handel went then to Hanover.

.   .   .   .   .   .

There were four brothers who became in turn
Dukes of Hanover : Christian Louis, George William,
John Frederick, and Ernest Augustus.[1] All four
were under the spell of France and Italy. They
passed the greater part of their time away from their
own States, choosing Venice for preference. George
William married morganatically a French lady of
the noble family of Poitou, Eléonora d'Olbreuse.
John Frederick was pensioned by Louis XIV, and
became Catholic. He took Versailles for his model,
and founded an Opera in 1672 at Hanover. He had
also the acumen to call Leibnitz into his States,[2]
but he took great care on his side that he should
remain there. He died in the course of a journey to
Venice. Ernest Augustus, who succeeded him, in
1680, was the patron of Steffani. He married the
beautiful and intelligent Duchess Sophia, a Palatine
princess, stepdaughter of James I Stuart, aunt of
the Palatine of France, and sister of the Princess
Elizabeth, friend of Descartes.[3] She herself was the

[1] See the book abounding in picturesque documents by
Georg Fischer, *Musik in Hannover*, Second Edition, 1903.

[2] In 1676, Leibnitz was then thirty years old. He received
the title of Councillor and President of the Library at the Castle.

[3] Moreover, by the quaintnesses of the Treaties of Westphalia,
this Protestant Princess found herself under the care of the
Catholic Bishop of Osnabruck.

E

friend and correspondent of Leibnitz, who admired
her. She had great intellectual gifts, spoke seven
languages, read widely, and had a natural taste for
the beautiful. " No one had greater gifts," said
Madame her niece, Michel de Montaigne. With
great lucidity of thought, decidedly outspoken, she
professed an epicurean materialism of great superiority and intelligence.[1] Her husband valued her
little, but he was brilliant and ostentatious. They
were the most polished and distinguished couple in
Germany at the Court of Hanover.[2] Both loved
music, but Ernest Augustus seems never to have
dreamt that it existed anywhere outside of Italy,
and he might almost as well have been called the
" Duke of Venice " as the Duke of Hanover, for he
was constantly in Venice, and never wished to leave
it for long.[3]

[1] Madame Arvède Barine has given an amusing portrait of
her, although a little severe, in her charming studies on *Madame
Mère du Regent*, 1909 (Hachette). See particularly the Memoirs
of the Duchess Sophia, written by the same author in French.

[2] Thus a French traveller, the Abbé Tolland, in 1702, expresses it.

[3] Created Duke in 1680, he left the same year for Venice. He
returned there at the end of 1684, and remained there until
about August, 1685. He returned three months later, in December, and only left it in September, 1686. He lived at the
palace Foscarini, with a numerous following, his ministers, his
poets, his musicians, his chapel. He spent enormous sums. He
gave *fêtes* to the Venetians, and took boxes by the year in five
theatres in Venice. In return he lent his subjects as soldiers to
Venice ; and his son, Maximilian, was a General in the Republic.
When the Grand Marshal of the Court of Hanover wrote to the
Prince of the discontent of his people, Ernest Augustus answered:
" I very much wish that Monsieur the Grand Marshal would
come here, then he would no longer write so often to me about
coming home. M. the Grand Marshal can have no idea how
amusing it is here, and if he only came once he would never
want to return to Germany."

The Hanover people began to murmur. The only means they could find of keeping their Prince at home with them was to build a magnificent opera house where spectacles and *fêtes* resembling those in Venice could be given. The idea was good. Ernest Augustus warmly took up the scheme for his opera house, which, built and decorated by the Italians between 1687 and 1690, was the most beautiful in all Germany.[1] For this opera house Steffani was engaged as Kapellmeister.[2] Agostina Steffani is one of the most curious figures in history.[3] Born in 1653 at Castelfranco, near Venice, of a poor family, after being a choir-boy at St. Mark's, he was taken in 1667 to Munich by the Count of Tattenbach, who had been the pupil of Ercole Bernabei, a master brought up in the purest Roman style.[4] At the same time he had been given a very complete education in literature, science, and theology, for he was destined for the priesthood, and

[1] Barthold Feind says in 1708 : " Of all the German opera houses, the Leipzig one is the poorest, that of Hamburg the largest, the Brunswick the most perfect, and that of Hanover the most beautiful." The Opera of Hanover had four tiers of boxes, and was capable of accommodating 1300 people.

[2] The orchestra was composed chiefly of French musicians, and they were conducted by a Frenchman, Jean Baptiste Farinel, son-in-law of Cambert.

[3] A. Einstein and Ad. Sanberger have just republished in the *Denkmäler der Tonkunst in Bayern* a selection of Steffani's works. Arthur Neisser has devoted a little book to Steffani. Apropos of one of his operas *Servio Tullio*, Leipzig, 1902. See also the studies of Robert Eitner in the *Allg. Deutsche Biographie ;* of Chrysander in his *Haendel* (Volume I), and also Fischer in his *Musik in Hannover.*

[4] Munich had become the centre of Italian music in Germany since the Prince-Elector Ferdinand had married in 1652 an Italian princess, Adelaide of Savoy. See Ludwig Schiedermair : *Die Anfange der Münchener Oper* (*Sammelb. der I.M.G.*, 1904).

with a view to becoming Abbé.[1] He was appointed
organist at the Court, and music-director. Since
1681 a set of his operas, played at Munich (and
especially *Servio Tullio* in 1685[2]), spread his renown
through Germany. The Duke of Hanover enticed
him to his Court, and in 1689 the new Hanoverian
theatre was inaugurated by one of Steffani's operas,
for which the Duchess Sophia furnished, it is said,
the patriotic subject *Henrico Leoni*.[3] Then followed
a set of fifteen operas of which the *mise en scène* and
music had an amazing popularity in Germany.[4]
Cousser introduced them at Hamburg as models
of true Italian song, and Keiser modelled himself partly on them, ten years before Handel in his
turn followed Keiser's pattern. The Opera did not
enjoy a long life at Hanover. The Duke alone
liked it. The Duchess Sophia had much less
sympathy for this kind of art.[5] The ballets and

---

[1] In 1680.

[2] One finds the list of Steffani's operas, together with an
analysis of the *Servio Tullio*, in the book of Arthur Neisser.

[3] This opera was played for the fifth centenary of the Siege
of Bardwick by Henry Lion-heart in 1089. The Elector of Brandenburg was at the first representation. Steffani treated other
German subjects, such as the *Tassilone* of 1709.

[4] The manuscripts of most of these operas are preserved in the
libraries of Berlin, Munich, London, Vienna, and Schwerin. It
is astonishing that they have never been published, notwithstanding their importance in the history of German opera.
Chrysander has given some specimens of the *libretti*. The music
has only been slightly studied by Neisser, who makes the mistake
of not knowing the music of the contemporaries of Steffani, and in
consequence is frequently at fault in his appreciation of him.

[5] Leibnitz neither, although he had certain intuition of what
was possible in this style of theatre-piece, which united all
the means of expression : beauty of words, of rhymes, of music,
of paintings, and harmonious gestures (letter of 1681). In
general he regarded music from the attitude of our Encyclo-

the masquerades put the Opera to shame. Steffani was otherwise occupied with more serious business elsewhere. In the Treaty of Augsburg, Ernest Augustus of Hanover had taken sides with the Emperor. To recompense his fidelity the Emperor bestowed on him the dignity of Prince-Elect, but in the confusion of the Empire it was not easy to clear up the situation. It was necessary to send an Ambassador Extraordinary to the great German Courts. The choice of all fell on Steffani, who, being a Catholic Abbé, could more easily serve as intermediary between the Protestant Court of Hanover and the Catholic Courts ;[1] his mission was so well accomplished that in 1697 the Duke of Hanover obtained for him the title of Elector. This astonishing diplomat had found the means of writing operas. After the death of Ernest Augustus in 1698 he gave up opera writing, but continued to occupy himself with politics. He became in 1703 the secret adviser to the Elector Palatine, the President of the Religious Council, who was created a noble. At the

pædists at the time of Rameau. His musical ideal was simple melody. " I have often remarked," says he, " that men of note have little esteem for things which are touching. Simplicity often makes more effect than elaborate ornaments " (letter to Henfling).

[1] The testimony of his contemporaries agrees in depicting him as a man of agreeable physique, small, of a debilious constitution, which the excess of study had aggravated, of a superior nature, but altogether lovable in his manners, full of wit and of gentleness, clear and calm in speech, possessing exquisite tact and perfect politeness, from which he never departed, an accomplished man of the court, and further very well informed, passionately interested in philosophy and mathematics. Leibnitz taught him German political law. We find in Fischer's *Musik in Hannover* a reproduction of a very rare portrait of Steffani in an episcopal costume.

same time Pope Innocent II made him in 1706
Bishop of Spiga.[1] The Elector Palatine created him
his Grand Almoner and gave him charge of the
Italian and Latin correspondence with the Duke of
Brunswick. From November, 1708, to April, 1709,
Steffani stayed at Rome, where the Pope crowded
honours on him, making him Prelate of the Chamber,
Assistant to the Throne, Abbé of St. Steffano in
Carrara, and Apostolic Vicar of the north of Germany,
with the supervision of the Catholics in Palatine,
Brunswick, and Brandenburg.[2] Then it was, as
we have seen, that he met Handel. It is necessary
to sketch briefly the life of this extraordinary
personage, who was at the same time Abbé, Bishop,
Apostolic Vicar, intimate Councillor and Ambassador of Princes, organist, Kapellmeister, musical
critic,[3] chief singer,[4] and yet composer—not only

[1] Bishop *in partibus*. Spiga was a district in the Spanish
West Indies.

[2] He ended by abdicating his post as Vicar, which cost him
more annoyance than pleasure. He travelled afresh in Italy in
1722. In 1724 he was nominated President for life of the Academy
of Ancient Music, founded in London by his pupil, Galliard. He
dedicated to the Academy several of his compositions, but since
he was made Bishop he no longer signed them ; they appeared
under the name of his secretary, Lagorio Piva. He returned to
Hanover in 1725, after having lived on a grander scale than his
revenues sufficed to maintain. He became embarrassed, and
had to sell his beautiful collection of pictures and statuary,
among which were found, it is said, some of Michael Angelo's.
The English king settled some of his debts. Steffani died of
apoplexy in the middle of a journey to Frankfort on February
12, 1728.

[3] A little work by him in the form of a letter is known. It is
entitled *Quanta certezza habbia de suoi Principii la Musica et in
qual pregio fosse perciò presso gli Antichi*, and was published in 1695
at Amsterdam. Again in 1700 in German. He therefore advanced
the value of music not only as an art, but also as a science.

[4] His singing was celebrated. If his voice was feeble, the

for the interest of his personality, but because he exercised considerable influence on Handel, who always retained a pleasant remembrance of him.

The feature in Steffani's art, and that by which he is superior to all of his own time, is his mastery of the art of singing. Well accustomed as all the Italians were to it, none wrote so purely for the voice as he. Scarlatti was not concerned with carrying the voice to its full limits, either for an expressive purpose or with a concerted intention. Thus in Steffani, as Hugo Goldschmidt says, " the singer held the pen." His work is the most perfect picture of Italian song in a golden age, and Handel owes to it his very refined feeling for the *bel canto*. In truth Steffani's operas gained little by this virtuosity. They were mediocre from the dramatic point of view, not very expressive, abused the vocalisation, and were essentially operas for singers.[1] They revealed a curious harmonic vein, and a contrapuntal alertness, which strongly contrasted with the nearly homophonic writing of Lully,[2] but the principal glory of Steffani was in his chamber vocal music, and especially in his duets.[3] These

purity and finish of his style, his delicate and chaste expression, were incomparable, if we are to believe Handel.

[1] They caused in truth a grand gathering of singers. *Servius Stallius* alone required twenty-five, of which six were sopranos (Nicer). *Op. cit.*

[2] On the other hand, the symphonic pieces, and particularly the overtures, are in the Lully style, and afforded the models for Handel. The French style reigned in the orchestra at Hanover. Telemann says, " at Hanover is the art of French science."

[3] Steffani seems to have written these duets as music master of the Court ladies, and several were composed for the Electress of Brandenburg, Sophia Dorothea. The poems were the work of the great lords, or the Italian Abbés. These duets were

duets are of various types, and of various lengths. One is a single piece. Others are in the *Da Capo* form. Some are veritable cantatas with recitatives, soli, and duets. Others are consecutive pieces, forming, as it were, little song-cycles. The writing in this form was evolved from Schütz and Bernabei to Handel and Telemann, but their inner construction is usually the same : the first voice announces alone the first phrase, which reflects the poetic emotion of the piece ; the second voice repeats the subject in the unison or in the octave ; with the second subject the voices leave the unison and indulge in canonic imitations which are freely treated. Then a return is made to the first part, which concludes the piece. When the duet is more developed, after the first air in the minor key, a second one comes in the major, where virtuosity is given free play, after which the minor air recurs. These works possess an admirable melodic beauty, and an expression often quite profound. In the lighter subjects Steffani has an easy gracefulness, the elegant fancy of Scarlatti. In his sad moments he reaches the highest models : from Schütz, from Provenzale, even to J. S. Bach. He is one of the greatest lyricists in the music of the seventeenth century.[1] These duets set the style in this form of

regarded in their time as masterpieces, and numerous copies were made of them. One finds the bibliography in the first volume of choice works of Steffani published by Breitkopf by A. Einstein and A. Zanberger. The Paris Conservatoire alone possesses six volumes of manuscript duets by Steffani.

[1] See the airs *Lungi dall' idol*, *Occhi perche piangete*, and particularly *Forma un mare*, which offer a striking analogy to one of the more beautiful *lieder* of Philip Heinrich Erlebach :

work. The *rôle* played by Steffani in music can very well be compared with that of Fra Bartolommeo in painting ;—both applied themselves with perfect art, and steadfast spirit, to find the laws of composition in limited and restrained forms : Fra Bartolommeo sought for the balance of groups, and the harmony of lines in scenes, with three or four persons grouped in a round picture ; Steffani concentrated all the efforts of his ingenuity, invention, and artistic science into the somewhat limited form of the duet. These two religious artists both have a luminous art ; both are sure of themselves, have learning and simplicity, with little or no passion. Their souls are noble, pure, a little impersonal. They were intended to prepare the way for others. As Chrysander says, " Handel walked in the steps of Steffani, but his feet were larger."

.   .   .   .   .   .

Handel made only a short stay at Hanover in 1710. Hardly had he taken up his duties when he asked and obtained leave to go to England, from whence proposals had been made to him. He crossed

Meine Seufzer (published by Max Friedlander in his History of the Song of the Eighteenth Century). There is every reason to believe that Steffani afforded one of the models for Erlebach.

One should notice the predilection of Steffani (like the great Italians of his time) for chromaticism and his contrapuntal taste. Steffani was one of the artists of the time nearest to the spirit of the ancient music, yet opening the way to the new, and it was characteristic that he was chosen as President of the Academy of Ancient Music of London, which took for its models the art of Palestrina and the Madrigalians of the end of the sixteenth century. I do not doubt that Handel learnt much, even in this, from Steffani.

Holland, and arrived at London at the end of the
autumn, 1710. He was then twenty-five years old.
The English musical era was broken off. Fifteen
years before, England had lost its greatest musician,
Henry Purcell, who died prematurely at the age of
thirty-six.[1]

In his short life he had produced a considerable
amount of work : operas, cantatas, religious music,
and instrumental pieces. He was a cultured genius,
and intimately acquainted with Lully, Carissimi,
and the Italian sonatas, at the same time very
English, possessing the gift of spontaneous melody,
and never losing contact with the spirit of the
British race. His art was full of grace and delicacy,
much more aristocratic than that of Lully. He
is the Van Dyck of music. Everything of his is
of extreme elegance, refinement, ease, slightly
exsangue. His art is natural : always steeped in
the country life which is indeed the source of the
English inspiration. There are no operas of the
seventeenth century where one finds fresher melodies
which are more inspired and yet of a popular
character. This charming artist was delicate, of
a weak constitution, somewhat feminine in character,
feeble, and of little stamina. His poetic languor
was his strongest appeal, and at the same time his
weak point ; he was prevented from following his
artistic progress with the tenacity of a Handel.
Most of his works lack finish. He never tried to
break down the final barriers which separated
him from perfection. His musical compositions

---

[1] Henry Purcell was born about 1658, and died in 1695.

are sketches of genius with strange weaknesses.
He produced many hastily finished operas with
singular awkwardnesses in the manner of treating
the instruments and the voice,—ill-fitting cadences,
monotonous rhythms, a spoilt harmonic tissue, and,
finally, in his larger pieces and those of grander
scale, there is a lack of breath, a sort of physical
exhaustion, which prevents him reaching the end
of his superb ideas. But it is necessary to take him
for what he is, one of the most poetic figures in
music—smiling, yet a little elegiac—a miniature
Mozart eternally convalescent. Nothing vulgar,
nothing brutal, ever enters his music. Captivating
melodies, coming straight from the heart, where
the purest of English souls mirrors itself. Full of
delicate harmonies, of caressing dissonances, a taste
for the clashing of sevenths and seconds, of incessant
poising between the major and minor, and with
delicate and varied nuances of a pale tint, vague
and slightly blurred, like the springtime sun piercing
through a light mist.[1] He only wrote one real opera,
the admirable *Dido and Æneas*, of 1680.[2] His
other dramatic works, very numerous, were music
for the stage, and the most beautiful type of this
kind is that which he wrote for Dryden's *King
Arthur* in 1691. This music is nearly all episodical.
One cannot remove it without causing the essential
action to suffer. The English taste was impatient

---

[1] See the Prelude or the Dance in *Dioclesian* and the overture
to *Bonduca*.

[2] English art has never produced anything more worthy of
being placed side by side with the masterpieces of the Italian
art than the scene of Dido's death.

of operas sung from one end to the other, and in
Handel's time Addison endeavoured to voice this
national repugnance in his *Spectator*.

It was a good thing that Handel had an altogether
different idea of opera, and that his personality
differed greatly from that of Purcell, which left him
no point for profiting (as he had done with others)
by the genius of his predecessor. Arriving in a
strange country, of which he did not even know
the language or the spirit, it was natural that he
should take the English master as his guide. Hence
the analogies between them. Purcell's Odes often
give one the impression of being merely a sketch
of the cantatas and oratorios of Handel. One finds
there the same architectural style, the same contrast
of movements, of instrumental colours, of large
ensembles, and of *soli*. Certain dances,[1] some of
the heroic airs, with irresistible rhythms and
triumphant fanfares,[2] are there already before
Handel, but they are only there as brilliant flashes
with Purcell. Both his personality and his art were
different. Like so many fine musicians of that time,
he has been swallowed up in Handel, just as a
stream of water loses itself in a river. But there was
nevertheless in this little spring a poetry peculiar
to England, which the entire work of Handel has
not—nor can have.

Since the death of Purcell the fount of English
music had dried up. Foreign elements submerged

[1] *King Arthur* : Grand Dance, or final Chaconne ; *Dioclesian* :
trio with final chorus.

[2] Particularly the famous song of St. George in *King Arthur*—
" St. George, the patron of our isle, a soldier and a saint."

it.[1] A renewal of Puritanical opposition which
attacked the English stage contributed to the dis-
couragement and abdication of the national artists.[2]
The last master of the great epoch, John Blow, an
estimable artist, famous in his time, whose personality is a little grey and faded, was not wanting in
distinction or in expressive feeling—but he had
then withdrawn himself into his religious thoughts.[3]

In the absence of English composers, the Italians
took possession of the field.[4] An old musician of
the Chapel Royal, Thomas Clayton, brought from
Italy some opera *libretti*, scores, and singers. He
took an old *libretto* from Boulogne, caused it to be
translated into English by a Frenchman, and
clumsily adapted it to music of little worth ; and,
such as it was, he proudly called it " The first
musical drama which has been entirely composed

[1] It was no longer French influence, which, very powerful at
the time of the Stuarts, had very nearly disappeared during the
Revolution of 1688 ; but the Italian.

[2] The celebrated pamphlet of the priest Jeremias Collier
appeared in 1688 : " A short view of the immorality and pro-
faneness of the English stage with the sense of Antiquity," had
made an epoch because it expressed with an ardent conviction
the hidden feelings of the nation. Dryden, the first, did humble
penitence.

[3] See the Preface to his *Amphion Britannicus* in 1700. Blow
died in 1708.

[4] There had been several efforts on the part of Italian opera
companies in London under the Restoration of 1660 and 1674.
None had succeeded, but certain Italians were installed in London, and had some success : about 1667 G. B. Draghi, about 1677
the violinist Niccolo Matteis, who spread the knowledge in English
of the instrumental works of Vitali and of Bassani ; the family
of Italian singers, Pietro Reggio de Gênes, and the famous Siface
(Francesco Grossi), who in 1687 was the first to give Scarlatti in
London ; Marguerita de l'Espine, who during 1692 gave Italian
concerts ; but it was in 1702 that the infatuation for the Italians
commenced.

and produced in England in the Italian style, *Arsinoé, Queen of Cyprus.*" This nullity, played at Drury Lane in 1705, had a great success, which even exceeded the authentic Italian opera given in the following year in London, *Camilla, regina de' Volsci*, by Marc Antonio Bononcini.[1] Vainly Addison tried to battle against the Italian invasion. By writing skits on the snobbism of the public with pleasant irony, he endeavoured to oppose the Italian Opera with a national English one.[2] He was defeated, and with him the entire English theatre collapsed.[3] " Thomyris " in 1707 inaugurated the representations half in Italian and half in English, and after the *Almahade* in January, 1710, all was in Italian. No English musician attempted to continue the struggle.[4]

When Handel arrived then, at the end of 1710,

---

[1] He was the brother of the celebrated Bononcini (Giovanni).

[2] This was *Rosamunde*, played in 1707, which had only three representations. Addison, very little of a musician, had taken as his collaborator the insipid Clayton. His satires against the Italian opera appeared in March and April, 1710, in the *Spectator*.

[3] The struggle was put into evidence in 1708, three years before the Haymarket Theatre was founded under the patronage of the Queen, by the poet Congreve, who gave there the old English plays. In 1708 the English drama left the place and opera installed itself.

[4] Two German musicians established in England, and naturalized, Dr. Christoph Pepusch and Nichilo Francesco Haym, pushed certain of their compositions on to the Italian opera stage in London. They were found there later. Pepusch, founder of the Academy of Ancient Music in 1710, was badly disposed against Handel, whose operas he ridiculed in the famous *Beggars' Opera* of 1728. Haym, who wished to publish in 1730 a great history of music, was one of Handel's librettists.

The Library of the Paris Conservatoire possessed a volume of airs from the principal Italian operas displayed in London from 1706 to 1710 (London, Walsh).

national art was dead. It would be absurd to say, as some have often done, that he killed English music. There was nothing left to kill. London had not a single composer. On the other hand, she was rich in excellent players. Above all she possessed one of the best troupes of Italian singers which could be found in Europe. Having been presented to the Queen Anne, who loved music, and played the clavier well, Handel was received with open arms by the Director of the Opera, Aaron Hill. He was an extraordinary person, who travelled in the East, wrote a history of the Ottoman Empire, composed tragedies, translated Voltaire, founded the " Beech Oil Company " for extracting the oil from the wood of the beech, mixing it with chemicals and using it for the construction of ships. This orchestral man composed during a meeting the plan of an opera, after *Jerusalem Delivered*. It was *Rinaldo*, which was written, poem and music, in fourteen days, and played for the first time on February 24, 1711, at the Haymarket.

Its success was immense. It decided the victory of the Italian Opera in London, and when the singer, Nicolini, who took the *rôle* of Renaud, left England he carried the score to Naples, where he had it produced in 1718, with the aid of young Leonardo Leo. The *Rinaldo* marked a turning-point in musical history. The Italian Opera, which had conquered Europe, began to be conquered in its turn by foreign musicians, who had been formed by it— the Italianised Germans. After Handel it was Hasse, then Gluck, and finally Mozart ; but Handel is the first of the conquerors.[1] After *Rinaldo*, and until the time when Handel had settled definitely in London, that is to say, between 1711 and the end of 1716, was an indecisive period which oscillated between Germany and England, and between religious music and the Opera.

Handel, who bore the title of Kapellmeister of Hanover, returned to his post in June, 1711.[2] At Hanover he found the Bishop Steffani again, and attempted to write in his style. In this imitation he composed some twenty chamber duets, which did not come up to their model, and some beautiful German songs on the poems by Brockes.[3] Several of his best instrumental pages, his first Oboe Concertos, his Sonatas for Flute and Bass,[4] seem to date from this time. The cavaliers of the Court of Hanover were ardent flautists, and the orchestra, under the direction of Farinel, was excellent ; especially had the oboes reached a high degree of virtuosity, which has hardly been approached at the present day. On the other hand, the Opera at Hanover was closed, and Handel could not even give *Rinaldo*.

He had a taste of the theatre, and did not like

[1] When the poet Barthold Feind gave in 1715 the translation of *Rinaldo* at Hamburg, he did not neglect to call him the universally celebrated Mr. Handel, known to the Italians as "*l'Orfeo del nostro secolo*" and "*un ingegno sublime*."

[2] He did not hurry. He stayed at Dusseldorf with the Elector Palatine (A. Einstein, etc., April, 1907), then in the later months of the year he went to see his family at Halle.

[3] To speak truly, they were more like little cantatas than *lieder*. The Collection Schoelcher in the Library of the Paris Conservatoire possesses these copies.

[4] Volumes XXVII and XLVIII of the Complete Handel Edition.

abandoning his plan; so he turned his eyes again towards London. Having tested the soil of England, and judged it favourable, Handel decided to establish himself there. He received regular news from England whilst in Hanover.[1] Since his departure no opera could hold its own except *Rinaldo*. The English amateurs recalled him, and Handel, burning to depart, asked for a new leave from the Court of Hanover. This was granted on the easiest of terms : " on condition that he returned after a reasonable time."[2]

He returned to London towards the end of November, 1712, in time to supervise the representation of a pastoral, *Il Pastor Fido*, a hasty work, from which he abstracted the best airs later on.[3] Twenty days later he had finished writing *Teseo*, a tragic opera in five very short acts,[4] full of haste and of genius, which was given in January, 1713.

Handel endeavoured to settle himself firmly in England. He associated himself with the loyalty and pride of the nation by writing for political celebrations. The conclusion of the Peace of Utrecht, a glorious day for England, approached. Handel prepared a *Te Deum*, which was already

[1] One sees by the letters of 1711 that Handel applied himself, even in Germany, to perfecting his knowledge of English.

[2] The House of Hanover was, as one knows, an aspirant for the succession to the throne of England, and it behoved it to keep on good terms with Queen Anne, who was partial to Handel.

[3] For his second version of this work in 1734 he then added some choruses.

[4] It is the only opera of Handel's which is in five acts. The poem was by Haym.

F

finished in January, 1713, but the laws of England forbade a foreigner to be charged with composing music for official ceremonies. Parliament alone could authorise the representation of this production. Handel cleverly wrote the flattering Ode for the anniversary of the birth of Queen Anne, *Birthday Ode of Queen Anne*. The Ode was performed at St. James's on February 6, 1713, and the Queen, enchanted with the work, commanded Handel to write the *Te Deum* and the *Jubilate* for the Peace of Utrecht, which was played on July 7, 1713, at a solemn service at St. Paul's, on which occasion the Members of Parliament attended. These works, in which Handel was helped by the example of Purcell,[1] were his first great efforts in the monumental style.

Handel had succeeded in securing, despite precedent, the post of Official Composer to the English Court. But he had not acted without grave neglect of his duties towards other masters, the princes of Hanover, in whose services he still was. The relationship was extremely strained between the cousin by heritage and her poor parents at Hanover. Queen Anne had taken a dislike to them, especially as she could not endure the intelligent Duchess Sophia. She made up songs about her, and dealt secretly with the Pretender Stuart, for whom she wished to secure the Heritage. In remaining in her service then, Handel took sides against his sovereign at Hanover. Certain historians have even breathed the word "treason." It is the

[1] Purcell had written in 1694 a *Te Deum* and *Jubilate*.

only fault which his biographer, Chrysander, does not excuse, for it wounded his German patriotism. But it is very necessary to say here that of German patriotism Handel had hardly any. He had the mentality of the great German artists of his time, for whom the country was art and religion ; the State mattered little to him.

He lived then amongst the English patrons—for a year with a wealthy music lover in Surrey—then in Piccadilly at Lord Burlington's palace. He remained there three years. Pope and Swift were familiars in the house, which Gay had described. Handel performed there on the organ and clavecin before the *élite* of London society by whom he was much admired—with the exception of Pope, who did not like music. He composed a little,[1] being satisfied to exist, as in his sojourn at Naples, waiting without hurry to be saturated by the English atmosphere. Handel was one of those who can write three operas in two months, and then do nothing more for a year. It is the rule of the torrential river which sometimes overflows, and then runs dry. He awaited the course of events. The inheritors of Hanover seemed decidedly ousted. The Duchess Sophia died on June 7, 1714, Chrysander says of grief (but it was certainly also apoplexy)—convinced that the Stuart would attain the coveted heritage. Less than ever did Handel breathe a word of returning to Hanover, but chance

[1] He wrote, it is said, for the little amateur theatre of Burlington an opera *Silla*, 1714, of which he reproduced the best parts in *Amadigi*. One can also date from this time a certain number of clavier pieces, which appeared in a volume in 1720.

upset all his plans. Two months after the death of the Duchess Sophia, Queen Anne died suddenly on August 1, 1714. The same day, in the confusion into which events had thrown the Stuart party, George of Hanover was proclaimed King by the secret council. On September 20 he arrived in London. He was crowned at Westminster on October 20, and Handel, very perturbed at the thought of his *Ode to Queen Anne*, had the mortification of seeing that had he waited another year his *Te Deum* would have served for the enthronement of the new dynasty.

To do him full justice, he did not seem much discomfited by this turn of fortune's wheel. He did not put himself about to ask for pardon. He set to work instead and wrote *Amadigi*. It was the very best way for him to plead his cause. George I of Hanover had many faults, but he had one good quality. He loved music sincerely, and this passion was shared by very many of the people more or less notable in his Court. Music had always been for Germany the fountain where soiled hearts purified themselves, the redemption from the petty basenesses of " the daily round, the common task." Whatever King George thought of Handel, he could not punish him without punishing himself. After the success of his charming *Amadigi*, played for the first time on May 25, 1715, he had not the courage to harbour malice any longer against his musician. They were reconciled.[1]   Handel resumed his post

[1] The legend records that Handel composed in August, 1715, the famous Water Music to regain the favour of the King.

GEORGE I., IN HIS ROYAL BARGE, LISTENING TO HANDEL'S "WATER-MUSIC."

(*From a Painting.*)

To face page 69.]

of Kapellmeister at Hanover by now acting as the music master to the little princesses, and when the King went to Hanover in July, 1716, Handel travelled with him.

It was not that he had much occupation at the Court. The King was too engrossed in State business, and with hunting. He did not even find time to be anxious about his old retainer, Leibnitz, who died at Hanover on November 14, 1716, unnoticed at Court. Handel took advantage of this leisure to renew his acquaintance with the German art.

There was then in Germany a fashion for musical Passions. There was a religious and theatrical tendency at that time. One cannot separate the influence of Pietism and that of the Opera. Keiser, Telemann, Mattheson, all wrote Passions, which caused a great stir[1] at Hamburg, on the famous

Installed on a boat, with a small " wind " orchestra, he had this work performed during one of the King's state processions on the Thames. The King was delighted, and renewed his friendship with Handel. Unfortunately, the Water Music appears to have been written two years later than the return to Court of Handel, and the scene placed by Chrysander on August 22, 1715, in his first volume—in October, 1715, by Fischer, *Musik in Hannover* —is changed by Chrysander in his third volume to July 17, 1717, with a cutting from one of the newspapers of that time, which does not seem, however, convincing to the others. Be that as it may, the work is from this period, and the first publication of it appeared about 1720.

[1] Keiser in 1712, *Der für die Sünden der Welt gemarterte und sterbende Jesus* (Jesus Crucified and Dying for the Sins of the World). Then Telemann in 1716, some months after Handel's arrival; a little later, Mattheson. Handel's *Passion* was executed for the first time at Hamburg during Lent 1717, when Handel had already returned to England. The four Passions of Keiser, Telemann, Mattheson, and Handel, were given in 1719 at the Hamburg Cathedral, Mattheson being choirmaster.

text of the Senator Brockes. Following their
example, perhaps in order to measure himself with
these men, who had all three been rivals or friends,[1]
Handel took the same text and wrote on it in 1716
his *Passion after Brockes*. This powerful and
disparate work, where bad taste mingles with the
sublime, where affectation and pomposity are
mingled with the most profound and serious art—
a work which J. S. Bach knew well, and very
carefully remembered—was for Handel a decided
experience. He felt in writing it what a great gulf
separated him from the Pietist German art, and on
his return to England[2] he composed the *Psalms* and
Esther.

•　　•　　•　　•　　•　　•

[1] Handel and Mattheson exchanged some correspondence.
Mattheson was about to engage in a musical polemic with the
organist and theorist, Buttstedt. He proved the need of building
on the sound foundations of the German music. He proposed
a suggestion for an enquiry on the Greek modes of Solmisation.
Handel, pressed on these questions, responded tardily in 1719 ;
he sided with Mattheson, a declared modernist against the old
modal period. Mattheson also asked for details of his life for
the purpose of including him in his biographical dictionary which
he had in view. Handel excused himself on account of the
concentration necessary. He merely promised in a vague
manner to relate later on the principal stages which he had taken
in the course of his profession, but Mattheson drew nothing more
from this source.

[2] At the end of 1716. In the course of this sojourn in
Germany, where he had assisted the widow of his former master,
Zachau, then fallen into great poverty, he also succoured at
Anspach an old University friend, Johann Christoph Schmidt,
who carried on a woollen business, and who left all—fortune,
wife, and child—to follow him to London. Schmidt remained
attached to Handel all his life, conducting his business affairs for
him, recopying his manuscripts, taking care of his music, and
afterwards his son, Schmidt (or Smith) Junior, took on the same
good offices with equal devotion, a striking instance of the
attractive powers which Handel excited on others.

This was the principal epoch of his life. Between 1717 and 1720, whilst he was in the service of the Duke of Chandos,[1] he made a careful examination of his own personality, and created a new style in music, and for the theatre.

The Chandos Anthems or Psalms[2] stand, in relationship to Handel's oratorios, in the same position as his Italian cantatas stand to his operas : they are splendid sketches of the more monumental works. In these religious cantatas, written for the Duke's chapel, Handel gives the first place to the choruses : it is the exact words of the Bible which they sing. Strong heroic words, freed from all the commentary and sentimental effusions with which German Pietism had loaded them. There is already in them the spirit and the style of *Israel in Egypt*, the great monumental lines, the popular feeling.

It was only a step from this to the colossal Biblical dramas. Handel took the step with *Esther*, which in its first form was entitled *Haman and Mordecai, a masque.*[3]

---

[1] The Duke of Chandos was a Crœsus, enriched in his office of Paymaster-General to the army in the reign of Queen Anne, and by his vast speculations in the South Sea Company. He built a magnificent castle at Cannons, a few miles from London. He had the *entourage* of a prince, and was surrounded by a guard of a hundred Swiss soldiers. His ostentation, indeed, was a little ridiculous. Pope made fun of it.

[2] The Anthems occupied three volumes of the Complete Handel edition. The third is reserved for the later works of this epoch, with which we are concerned here. The two first volumes contained eleven Chandos anthems, of which two have a couple of versions and one has three. Handel wrote at the same time three *Te Deums.*

[3] Masques were secular compositions very much in the fashion in England at the time of the Stuarts. They were part

Quite possibly the work had its first presentation at the Duke of Chandos', but on August 29, 1720, it was presented on the stage. It was in any case one of the greatest tragedies in the old style which had been written since the Grecian period. It was as though the spirit of Handel had been led insensibly towards the Hellenic ideal, for he composed nearly at the same time his pastoral tragedy *Acis and Galatea*, to which he also gave the name of masque,[1] and which did not disengage itself from the complete idea of a free theatre. This little masterpiece of poetry,[2] and of music, where the beautiful Sicilian legend unfolds itself in pictures smiling and mournful, has a classical perfection which Handel never surpassed.

.   .   .   .   .   .

Esther and *Acis* bore witness to Handel's desire to bring to the surface of dramatic action all the powers of choral and symphonic music. Even in these two works, which unquestionably opened up the way for his future oratorios, it is not the oratorio which is his aim, but the opera. Always attracted by the theatre, only a succession of disasters of accumulating ruin thrust him away

played and part danced, as theatre plays, and partly sung as concert pieces (see Paul Reyher : *Les*, etc., Paris, 1909).

Handel took up his *Esther* in 1732 and recast it. The first *Esther* had a single part, it comprised six scenes. The second *Esther* had three acts, each preceded and terminated by a full chorus in the ancient manner. Some have asserted that the poem was by Pope.

[1] Later on, when he took up this work again in 1733, he called it an English opera.

[2] The pretty poem is by Gay.

later against his will. So it is natural to find him at the same time when he was writing *Esther* and *Acis*, also undertaking the musical direction of a theatre enterprise, which led later on to one of the most important steps of his life, the Academy of Italian Opera.[1]

Handel saw, it is said, in the year 1720 the end of his years of apprenticeship ; he certainly terminated (although he knew it not) his years of tranquillity. Up to then he had led the life of numberless other great musicians, who lived under the protection of princes, and wrote for a select audience. He had only occasion to leave this path, with his religious and national works, where he had voiced a people's feelings. After 1720, and indeed up to the time of his death, all the rest of his art belonged to everybody. He put himself at the head of a theatre, and opened a struggle with the public at large. He exerted prodigious vitality, writing two or three operas every year, knocking into shape an undisciplined troupe of *virtuosi* smothered with pride, harassed with intrigues, hindered by bank-

---

[1] This was a society with a capital of £50,000 by shares of £100 subscribed for fourteen years, each share giving the use of one seat in the theatre. At the head of it, as President, was the Lord Chamberlain, Duke of Newcastle. (Until 1723, when he entered the Ministry, and was replaced by the Duke of Grafton.) The second President, the real director, was Lord Bingley. He was assisted on the Council of Administration by twenty-four directors re-elected yearly. The whole scheme was under the protection of the King, who paid £1000 a year for his box. The dividends paid to the shareholders reached in 1724 7%, but speculation endangered the work, and indeed led to its ruin.

Handel was charged with the complete musical direction until 1728, when he took on his shoulders the whole direction of the opera, financial and musical.

ruptcy, using his genius for twenty years in the paradoxical task of thrusting on London a shaky and shallow Italian opera, which could not live under a sun and in a climate unsuitable to it. At the end of this strife, enraged, conquered, but invincible, sowing on his way all his masterpieces, he reached the pinnacle of his art—those grand oratorios which rendered him immortal.

After a voyage in Germany to Hanover, to Halle, to Düsseldorf, and to Dresden, to recruit for his troupe of Italian singers,[1] Handel inaugurated at the Haymarket Theatre the London Opera of April 27, 1720, with his *Radamisto*, which was dedicated to the King.[2] The rush of the public was very great indeed, but it was due more to curiosity than to the turn of the fashion. Soon the snobbishness of the amateurs could no longer content itself with Italianized German as the representative of Italian Opera, and finally Lord Burlington, Handel's former patron, went to Rome to induce the king of the Italian style, Giovanni Bononcini, to come over.[3]

Bononcini came from Modena. He was about fifty years old,[4] son of an artist of great merit,

[1] This voyage took place from February, 1719, to the end of the same year. When Handel was staying at Halle, J. S. Bach, who was then at Cothen, about four miles away, was informed of it, and went there to see him, but he only arrived at Halle the very day when Handel was about to leave. Such at least is the story of Forkel.

[2] The poem was by Haym. From 1722 the work was given at Hamburg with a translation of Mattheson.

[3] Before him Domenico Scarlatti had already visited London, where he had given unsuccessfully an opera, *Narcissus*, 1720.

[4] He was born in 1671 or 1672, for his first opus appeared in 1684 or 1685, when he was little more than thirteen years old. Giovanni Bononcini was far from being well known. He was

Giovanni Bononcini, whose premature death cut short a career rich with promise.[1] Brought up with an almost paternal affection by one of the first masters of that epoch, one of the few who had preserved the cult and the science of the past, Giampaolo Colonna, organist of St. Pietronio at Bologna, he had benefited early in life by a high princely, even Imperial,[2] protection. More precocious even than Handel, he published his first works at the age of thirteen, was member of the Philharmonic Academy of Bologna at fourteen, and master of the Chapel at fifteen. His first works were instrumental. This was his speciality, having inherited his gift from his father.[3] He only reached the Opera after having tried all the other styles. It was not with him a natural calling. He was a born

not a celebrated musician, on which account there are many disagreements. Bononcini was the name of a long string of musicians, and one has been frequently confounded with the other. Such mistakes are found even in the critical work of Eitner (where they rest on a great error in reading) and in the most recent Italian works, as that of Luigi Torchi, who in his instrumental music in Italy, 1901, confounds all the Bononcini together. Luigi Francesco Valdreghi's monograph *I Bononcini in Modena*, 1882, is more reliable, although very incomplete.

[1] Gianmaria Bononcini was Chapel-Master of the Cathedral of Modena, and attached to the service of Duke Francis II. A fine violinist, author of instrumental sonatas in suites, to which Mr. Torchi and Sir Hubert Parry attribute great historical importance. He had a reflective spirit, and dedicated in 1673 to the Emperor Leopold I a treatise on Harmony and Counterpoint, entitled *Musico Practico*, which was afterwards reprinted. He died in 1678, less than forty years old.

[2] Several of his early works are dedicated to Francis II of Modena, and his 8th opus, *Duetti da Camera*, 1691, is dedicated to the Emperor Leopold I, who caused him to be engaged for the Court Chapel.

[3] He was a celebrated violoncellist.

concert musician, and he remained so even in the Opera. His tours in Germany and in Austria, where he was created Imperial Composer in 1700, and gave his *Polifemo* at Berlin in 1703,[1] fully established his renown in Europe. His music spread in France after 1706 and excited there an almost incredible infatuation.[2] When in Italy his reputation surpassed even that of Scarlatti, who himself, according to Mr. Dent, came under his influence to a small extent. He had a European vogue for about ten or fifteen years. He was, so to speak, the reflection of the society of his time.

What strikes one in his music, if we are to believe Lecerf de la Viéville, is the boldness of his modulations, the abundance of his vocal ornaments, the unruliness of his mind. His style seemed to the Lullyists that of the affected and distorted order as opposed to the school of common sense. Bononcini was a " verticalist " then, differing from the " horizontalists" of the preceding epoch.[3] He was essentially a sensuous musician, and an anti-intellectualist. Right from the beginning, as an instrumental composer he always remained indifferent to his poems, to his subjects, and to everything which was outside of music. In his music he set a pleasing sonority

---

[1] Alfred Ebert : *Attilo Ariosto in Berlin*, 1905, Leipzig.

[2] See Lecerf de la Viéville : *Eclaircissement sur Bononcini*, published in the 3rd part of his *Comparaison de la musique française avec la musique italienne* (1706).

[3] " Like Corelli," says Lecerf, " he had a few fugues, contra fugues, based on conceits, frequently in other Italian works, and he made many delicious things from all the lesser used intervals, the most valiant and the most strange. His dissonances struck fear."

above everything ; [1] and it was evidently on this
account that his work required less effort of the
intelligence than was necessitated by the severe
art of Scarlatti, or the recitative and expressive art
of Lully.[2] In him was inaugurated the reaction of
fashionable good taste in the general public against
that of the savant.[3] Contrast the grand airs *Da
Capo*, broadly developed in a more or less contrapuntal fashion, with his tiny little airs, also *Da Capo*,
but in miniature, easy to understand, which touched
the popular feeling for melody. He carefully
perfumed it and served it up for the taste of the
elegant and fashionable.[4] This distinguished simplicity, this delicate sensibility, rather feeble,
always so correct in its audacities and restrained in
its pleasures, made Bononcini a drawing-room
favourite, a fashionable revolutionary. The more he

---

[1] See the gentle suspension of notes in the Cantata *Dori e
Aminta* (manuscript in the Library of the Conservatoire of Paris),
or the Cantata *Care luci* (*ibid.*).

[2] " What is necessary in music," said *The London Journal*
of February 24, 1722, " is that it should chase away *ennui*, and
relieve clever men from the trouble of thinking."

[3] It is the eternal struggle between the art of knowledge and
the pseudo-popular art. It recurred again a little later with
Rousseau. The principal difference between the two phases of
the strife is that in the epoch with which we are occupied the
champion of the anti-learned art was a well-instructed musician
who did not uphold his cause by ignorance, but by laziness and
by profligacy.

[4] " To study this more closely," says Hugo Goldschmidt (*Vocal
Ornamentation*, 1908), " Bononcini's songs are really *lieder*, to
which is applied, for good or evil, the old form of the Aria Da
Capo, or the Cavatina : the taste for little airs in the form of a
song spread itself widely during the end of the seventeenth century
in Germany and in England." Bononcini, who was always led
naturally by fashion, and by his indolent facility, abandoned
himself to it still more in England, and suited it to the English
taste.

worked, the more his traits were accentuated, and became permanent. As happens to all artists who enjoy too much success, this reacted on his art, and imposed on him the repetition of certain fixed patterns. The natural laziness of Bononcini only exaggerated this tendency, so that from year to year this affectedness appeared in his art, making it quite mechanical. His music, often beautiful and gracious, always harmonious, never expressive, unrolled itself as a succession of elegant and highly finished subjects, all cut out as if with scissors on the same pattern, and indefinitely repeated. At first in London one was only conscious of his charm. The personality of the musician added to the attractions of his music. The gentle Italian had polished manners, a quality at once lovable, and penetrated by a bold courage. He was a *virtuoso* like Handel, but on an instrument more distinguished than the clavier—on the violoncello ; and he was listened to with respect in the aristocratic *salons*. He was, so to speak, the author *à la mode ;* and his *Astarto*,[1] given at the end of 1720, erased the impression made by Handel's *Radamisto*.

Handel had his work cut out. He was not suited to strive with Bononcini on the ground of Italianism. However, he was up against the wall. The English public, always keen on bear fights, cock fights, and *virtuoso* contests, amused themselves by arranging

---

[1] The work had already been given in Italy about 1714. It was then that Lord Burlington heard it, and became the champion of Bononcini when he decided to come to England.

a joust between Bononcini and Handel. They were
to be tested by an opera written in combination.
Handel took up the glove—and was beaten. His
Muzio Scevola[1] (March, 1721) is very feeble, and
the *Floridante* which followed (December 9, 1721)
is little better. The success of the Italian increased
his fame, and the pretty *Griselda* (February, 1722)
consummated Bononcini's glory. He benefited by
the strenuous opposition of the English *littérateurs*,
and the leading aristocrats, against the Hanoverian
Court and the German artists.

Handel's situation was much involved, but he
took his revenge with the melodious opera *Ottone*
(January 12, 1723), which was the most popular of
all his operas. Victorious then,[2] he went straight
ahead without troubling himself about Bononcini,
and he composed, one after another, three masterpieces in which he inaugurated a new musical
theatre, as musically rich, and more dramatic than
that of Rameau, some ten years later: *Guilio
Cesare* (February 20, 1724); *Tamerlano* (October

[1] Handel wrote the third act, Bononcini the second, the
first had been already set by a certain Signor Pippo (Phillipo
Matti ?).

[2] The victory of Handel began for the most part with the
engagement of his new interpreter, Francesca Cuzzoni, of Parma,
a great and vigorous artist, violent and passionate, whose excellent soprano voice excelled particularly in pathetic *cantabile*
music. She was twenty-two years old, and came to London,
where she made her début in *Ottone*. Her quarrels with Handel,
and how he treated her by threatening to throw her out of the
window, are well known.

Handel gave again in May another opera, *Flavio*, of little
importance. On his side Bononcini produced *Erminia and
Attilio, Aristosi, Coreolanus*, in which the prison scene reduced
the ladies to tears, and inspired numerous analogous scenes in
the following operas of Handel.

21, 1724), and *Rodelinda* (February 13, 1725). The last of *Tamerlano* is a magnificent example of the great music drama, an example nearly unique before Gluck, in its poignancy and passion. Bononcini's party was definitely ruined,[1] but the greatest difficulties now began for Handel. The London Opera was delivered over into the hands of *Castrati* and *Prime Donne*, and the extravagances of their supporters. In 1726 there arrived the most celebrated Italian singer of the time, the famous Faustina.[2] From this moment the London representations became mere jousts of song between Faustina and Cuzzoni—jousts as strenuous as the shouting of their various partisans. Handel wrote his *Alessandro* (May 5, 1721) for an artistic duel between the two stars of his troupe, who acted as the two mistresses of *Alessandro*.[3] In spite of all, his dramatic genius won the day by several sublime scenes from *Almeto* (January 31, 1727), the grandeur of which veritably seized hold of the public. But the rivalry of the singers, far from being appeased, redoubled in fury. Each party had its hired pamphleteers, who let loose on the adversary the

[1] Bononcini gave his last piece, *Kalfernia*, on April 18, 1724. Ariosti says possibly in 1725. On the other hand, in 1725 there commenced to be played in London the works of Leonardo Vinci, and Porpora, patronized by Handel himself.

[2] Faustina Bordoni was born in 1700 at Venice. She had been educated in the school of Marcello. In 1730 she married Hasse. Her singing had an incredible agility. No one could repeat the same note with such rapidity, and she seemed able to hold on sounds to any extent. Less concentrated and less profound than Cuzzoni, she had an art more moving and brilliant.

[3] Two months before Handel had given the opera *Scipione* (March 12, 1726).

most degrading libels. Cuzzoni and Faustina reached such a state of rage that on June 6, 1727, during the play, they fought and tore each other's hair unmercifully, amidst the yells of the audience, the Princess of Wales being present.[1]

After this everything went to the dogs. Handel tried hard to take the reins, but, as his friend Arbuthnot said, " the devil was loose, and could never be caged again." The battle was lost, despite three new works of Handel, where his genius again shone forth : *Riccardo I* (November 11, 1727) ; *Siroe* (February 17, 1728) ; and *Tolomeo* (April 30, 1728). A little venture by John Gay and by Pepusch, *The Beggar's Opera* (A War Opera) finished the defeat of the London Academy of Opera.[2] This excellent operetta, spoken in dialogue, with popular songs interspersed, was at the same time a trenchant satire on Walpole, and a spirited parody of the ridiculous sides of the opera.[3] Its immense success

[1] The Director of the Drury Lane Theatre, Colley Cibber, produced, a month later, a farce called *The Contretemps, or The Rival Queens*, where the two singers were depicted tearing their chignons, and Handel saying in anger to them, whom he wished to separate, " Leave them alone, when they are tired their fury will spend itself out," and, in order that the strife might be definitely finished, he wound it up with great strokes on the drum. Handel's friend, Dr. Arbuthnot, also published on this subject one of his best pamphlets, " The Devil let loose at St. James's " (see Chrysander, Volume II).

[2] The last representation at the Academy took place on June 1, 1728, with *Almeto*.

[3] Amongst others, the accompanied recitative, the air *Da Capo*, the opera duets, the farewell scenes, the great prison scenes, the inconsequent ballads. Pepusch even took an air of Handel and parodied it. In the second act a band of robbers came together in the tavern, and solemnly defiled before their chiefs to the sound of the March of the Crusaders' Army in

took the character of a national manifestation. It was a reaction of popular common sense against the pompous childishnesses of the Italian Opera, and against the snobbishness which attempted to impose it on other nations. We see in this the first blow struck at the triumphant Italianism. Nationality awoke. In 1729 the *Passion according to St. Matthew* was given. Some years later Handel's earlier oratorios were performed, and also the first operas of Rameau. In 1728 to 1729 Martin Heinrich Fuhrmann entered the campaign against Italian Opera with his famous pamphlets. After him, Mattheson re-entered the ring : *The Goths and their Hippogriffs to be purified in the crater of Etna*. But nowhere was this national reaction so widely spread as in England, where it roused itself with such robust humour, as with Swift and with Pope, those famous layers of ghosts[1] and dreams.

.   .   .   .   .   .

Handel felt this. After 1727 he sought steadily to establish himself on the national English soil. He had become a naturalized Englishman on February 13, 1726. He wrote for the Coronation of

Rinaldo—The Beggar's Opera, given for the first time on January 29, 1728, was played all over England, and aroused violent polemics. Swift became a passionate champion for it. After the success appeared in the following years a number of operas with songs—Georgy Kalmas has dedicated a very complete article to *The Beggar's Opera* in his *Sammelbände der I.M.G.* (January to March, 1907).

[1] The first three books of the *Dunciad* of Pope appeared in 1728 ; *The Voyages of Gulliver* in 1726. Swift did not forget the musical folly in his satire on the kingdom of Lilliputia.

the new King, George II, his Coronation Anthems,[1] September 11, 1727.[2] He returned to his plans for the English oratorios.

But he was not yet sufficiently sure of his ground, nor of the public taste, to justify him in completely throwing over the Italian Opera, for he realized more than before the resources of the people and what he could do with them. Besides, the collapse of the London Academy of Opera had not touched his personal prestige. He was regarded, not only in England, but also in France, as the greatest man of the Lyric Theatre.[3] His London Italian operas became known all over Europe.

> *Flavius, Tamerlan, Othon, Renaud, César,*
> *Admete, Siroé, Rodelinde, et Richard,*
> *Éternels monumens dressés à sa mémoire,*
> *Des operas Romains surpassèrent la gloire,*
> *Venise lui peut-elle opposer un rival ?*[4]

One can well understand, then, that Handel was tempted by the desire of taking on his own shoulders, without the control which hampered him, the complete enterprise of the Italian Opera. At the end of the summer of 1728 he went to Italy in search of new

[1] The Coronation Anthems comprised four hymns, of which we do not know the exact order. Handel arranged for their presentation at Westminster by forty-seven singers, and a very considerable orchestra.

[2] *Riccardo I*, played in November of the same year (see p. 81), was also a national opera, dedicated to King George II, and celebrating, *apropos* of Richard Cœur de Lion, the annals of Old England.

[3] See page 48, note 4, the opinions held by Séré de Rieux.

[4] Séré de Rieux : *les Dons les enfants de Latone ; la Musique et la Chasse du cerf*, poems dedicated to the King, 1734, Paris, p. 102–3.

arms for the strife. In the course of this tour, which lasted nearly a year,[1] he recruited his singers, renewed his collection of *libretti* and Italian scores. Above all, he refreshed his Italianism at the source of the new School of Opera, founded by Leonardo Vinci,[2] which reacted against the concert style in the theatre, and sought to give back to Opera a more dramatic character, even at the risk of impoverishing the music.

Without sacrificing the richness of his style, Handel did not neglect to profit by these examples in his new operas : *Lotario* (December, 1729), *Partenope* (February, 1730), *Poro* (February, 1731), *Ezio* (January, 1732), which are notable (particularly the last two) by the beauty of the melodic writing, and the dramatic power of certain pages. The masterpiece of this period is *Orlando* (January 27, 1733), of which the richness and musical perfection are on a level with the insight into the characters, and the spirited and passionate life of the piece. If the *Tamerlano* of 1724 awakens ideas of Gluck's tragedies, it is the beautiful operas of Mozart which come to mind in *Orlando*.

---

[1] During this voyage, where he sojourned a considerable time at Venice, he learned that his mother was stricken with paralysis. He hastened to Halle, so that he might see her again, but she could no longer see him. For several years she had been blind. She died the following year, December 27, 1730. Whilst Handel was at Halle watching over his mother, he received a visit from Wilhelm Friedemann Bach, who came on behalf of his father, to invite him to come to Leipzig. One can well understand that Handel declined the invitation under his sad circumstances.

[2] Born in 1690 at Strongoli in Calabria, he died in 1730. He was the master of the Chapel Royal at Naples, where he preceded Pergolesi and Hasse. I have spoken of Vinci in another volume.

In continuation of the strife for the Italian Opera, Handel profited by the unexpected success with which the English people had met the reproduction of his *Acis and Galatea* and his *Esther*,[1] written to English words, and he attempted again, in a more conscientious fashion than ten years before at Chandos', to found a form of musical theatre, freer and richer, where the lyricism of the choruses had free play. For the reproduction of *Esther* in 1732 he introduced into the work of 1720 the most beautiful choruses from the Coronation Anthems. In the following year he wrote *Deborah* (March 17, 1733, and *Athaliah* (July 10, 1733), where the chorus took first place. These grand Biblical dramas would have been able to have awakened in the English nation an enthusiastic response, were it not that this attempt was damaged by a violent quarrel inspired by personal reasons, where art counted for nothing. A dead set was made against *Deborah*,[2]

---

[1] *Acis and Galatea* was reproduced in 1731, then given again in 1732, at the Haymarket Theatre, with the scenery and costumes, under the title of *An English Pastoral Opera*. The representation had taken place without the consent of Handel, who in response to the event, gave the work himself a little later. As for *Esther*, a member of the Academy of Ancient Music, Bernard Gates, who had formerly sung in the piece at the Duke of Chandos' and who possessed a copy of it, produced it at the Hostelry of the Crown and Anchor, on February 23, 1732. In his turn Handel directed the work on May 2, 1732, at the Haymarket Theatre, under the title of English *Oratorio*. These presentations did not appease the interest of the public.

[2] In the " first place there were in all," said a pamphlet, " 260 persons, of whom many had free tickets, and others were even paid to come." Handel tried to give the work again at reduced prices. This brought him no advantage. The English patrons repeated already their exultation over the Saxon, and caused him to return to Germany.

and though *Athaliah* succeeded at Oxford,[1] Handel
did not present it in London until two years
later.

Once again Handel returned to Italian Opera.
The public hatred pursued him here also. The royal
family of Hanover was detested. It added to its
own discredit by the scandalous disputes which
took place between the King and his son. The
Prince of Wales, in a spirit of petty spite against his
father, who showed his affection for Handel, amused
himself by attempting to ruin the composer.
Encouraged by the opposition, and enchanted by
the idea of making sport against the King, he
founded a rival opera house, and as he could no
longer set Bononcini up against Handel, as the
former had been discredited by a case of flagrant
plagiarism, which had an European circulation,[2] he

[1] *Athaliah* was written for the University feasts at Oxford,
to which Handel had been invited. They wished to confer on
him there the title of Doctor of Music. One does not know
exactly what happened to Handel, having always refused the
honour. It is certain, however, that Handel did not receive the
title.

[2] Bononcini had been received into the Academy of Ancient
Music at London. To secure his footing he offered the Academy
in 1728 a Madrigal in five voices. Unfortunately for him, three
years after, a member of the Academy found this Madrigal in a
book of duets, trios, madrigals of Antonio Lotti, published in
1705 at Venice. Bononcini persisted in claiming the authorship
of the work. A long enquiry was instituted, in which Lotti
himself and a great number of witnesses were examined. The
result was disastrous for Bononcini, who threw up all and disappeared from London towards the end of 1732—the whole of
the correspondence relating to this affair was published by the
Academy in Latin, Italian, French and English, under the title
" Letters from the Academy of Ancient Music at London to
Signor Antonio Lotti of Venice, with answers and testimonies,
London, 1732."

approached Porpora, with a view to directing his theatre. " Then," says Lord Hervey, " the struggle became as serious as that of the Greens against the Blues at Constantinople under Justinian. An anti-Handelian was regarded as an anti-Royalist, and in Parliament, to vote against the Court was hardly more dangerous than to speak against Handel." On the other hand, the immense unpopularity of the King redounded on Handel, and the aristocracy combined to secure his downfall.

He accepted the challenge, and after a third tour in Italy during the summer of 1733, again to recruit more singers, he bravely took up the fight with Porpora, to whom was added Hasse in 1734. They were the greatest rivals against which he had yet measured himself. But Hasse and Porpora had strong dramatic feeling, and especially were they the most perfect masters of the beautiful art of Italian melody and singing.[1] Nicolo Porpora, who came from Naples, was forty-seven years old. He had a cold but vigorous spirit, intelligent and possessing more than anyone else, except Hasse, all the resources of the Italian singing. His style was very beautiful, and it was not less broad than that of Handel. No other Italian musician of his time had such ample breadth of phrasing.[2] His writings seem of a later age than Handel's, and approximate

---

[1] Porpora was the most famous Italian teacher of singing of the eighteenth century. Hasse was himself a great singer, and married one of the most celebrated Prima Donnas who ever lived, Faustina.

[2] Contrast with the short and restricted phrases of Benedetto Marcello in his *Arianna*, the amplitude of Porpora's treatment of the same subject.

to the time of Gluck and Mozart. Whilst Handel, despite his marvellous feeling for plastic beauty, often treated the voices as an instrument, and in his development the beautiful Italian lines occasionally became weighed down by German complexity, Porpora's music always kept within the bounds of classic purity, though the form was a little uninteresting in design. History has never done him sufficient justice.[1] He was quite worthy of measuring himself against Handel, and the comparison between Handel's *Arianna* and that of Porpora, played at an interval of a few weeks,[2] did not prove to the advantage of the former. Handel's music is elegant, but one does not find the breadth of certain airs in Porpora's *Arianna à Naxos*. The form of these airs is perhaps of too classic a correctness, but the right Grecian breezes blow across his Roman temples.[3] He has been claimed as an Italian disciple of Gluck—a curious criticism which is bestowed occasionally on precursors. It was so with Jacopo della Quercia, who inspired Michael Angelo, and to whom the latter seems to owe something.

Hasse was even superior to Porpora in the charm of his melody, which Mozart alone has equalled, and in his symphonic gifts, which showed themselves in his rich instrumental accompaniments no less

[1] Chrysander, who did not know him well, speaks with a disdain absolutely unjustifiable.

[2] Handel's *Arianna*, January 26, 1734. Porpora's *Arianna à Naxos*, a little later.

[3] Thus the Invocation of Theseus to Neptune : *Nume che reggi'l mare*, and the air : *Spetto d' orrore*.

melodious than his songs.[1] Handel was not slow
to discover the folly of striving with Hasse on
Italian ground. His superiority was with the
choruses ; he sought to introduce them into the
Opera after the French model. The situation was
even less promising for him on the departure of his
best protectrix, the Princess Anne, sister of the
Prince of Wales.[2] After having compromised
Handel by the strong feeling which she had shown
in defending him, she left him to the tender cares
of the enemies which she had made for him. She
left England in April, 1734, to join her husband
the Prince of Orange[3] in Holland.

Handel came to be abandoned by his old friends.
His associate, Heidegger, the proprietor of the
Haymarket Theatre, took the hall for a rival opera,

---

[1] Johann Adolf Hasse was born March 23, 1699, at Bergedorf,
near Hamburg, and died on December 16, 1783, at Venice. He
came to London in October, 1734, where he gave his *Artaserse*,
which was played until about 1737. He also gave in England
his *Siroé*, 1736, and two comic *intermezzi*. I do not attach much
importance to him, for his life and his art are a little outside
the scope of this work. Despite the efforts of Handel's enemies,
Hasse always avoided posing as the rival of his great country-
man, and their art remains independent of each other. I
will hold over (till some time later on) the study of the work of
this admirable artist, for posterity has been even more unjust
to him than to Porpora, for no one had his wonderful sense of
melodic beauty in such a degree, and in his best pages he is the
equal of the very greatest.

[2] She was Handel's pupil and friend. An excellent musician,
she conducted the orchestra at public concerts given by her
every evening in Holland.

[3] Handel composed for the marriage of the Princess Anne
The Wedding Anthem (March 14, 1734), which is a *pasticcio* of
old works, especially *Athaliah*. He gave also for the marriage
fêtes the serenata, *Parnasso in festa*, and a revised form of
Pastor Fido, with choruses.

and Handel, driven from the house in which he had worked for fourteen years, had to emigrate with his troupe to John Rich's place at Covent Garden[1]—a sort of music-hall where Opera took its turn with all kinds of other spectacles : ballets, pantomimes, and harlequinades. In Rich's troupe some French dancers were to be found, amongst whom was " *la Salle*,"[2] who was shortly to arouse great enthusiasm amongst the English public with two tragic dances : *Pygmalion* and *Bacchus and Ariadne*.[3] Handel, who had known the French art[4] for a long time, saw how far he could draw on these new resources, and he opened the season of 1734 at Covent Garden with a first attempt in the field of the French ballet opera : *Terpsichore* (November 9, 1734), in which " *la Salle* " took the principal *rôle*. A month later a *Pasticcio* followed, *Orestes*, where Handel gave a similar important part to " *la Salle*," and to her expressive dances. Finally, he intermingled the dance and the choruses closely with the dramatic action in two masterpieces of poetry and beautiful

[1] It was John Rich who had produced here the *Beggar's Opera* of Gay and Pepusch in 1728—that parody of Handel's operas.

[2] She was the pupil of Mlle Prévost, and made her début in 1725 with Rich. See the study of M. Emile Dacier : *Une danseuse française à Londres, au début du XVIII siècle* (French number of the S.I.M. May and July, 1907).

[3] It is interesting to notice that it was with the same subjects of *Pygmalion* and of *Ariadne* that J. J. Rousseau and Georg Benda inaugurated in 1770–1775 the Melodrama or " opera without singing."

[4] He has been accused of knowing it too well. The Abbé Prevost wrote exactly at this same period in *Le Pour et le Contre* (1733) : " . . . Certain critics accuse him of having taken for his basis an infinite number of beautiful things from Lully, and especially from our French cantatas, and of having the effrontery of disguising them in the Italian manner. . . ."

·musical construction—*Ariodante* (January 8, 1735), and especially *Alcina* (April 16, 1735).

Bad luck still pursued him. Some gross national manifestations compelled *"la Salle"* and her French dancers to leave London.[1] Handel gave up the ballet opera. To leave at this moment, if he was to continue the struggle with the theatre, went badly against the grain, and was tantamount to declaring himself vanquished. At the opening of his theatrical enterprise he had saved, so it is said, £10,000. All this was absorbed, and already he was £10,000 more to the bad. His friends did not understand his obstinacy, which seemed about to involve him in complete ruin. " But," says Hawkins, " he was a man of intrepid spirit, and in no ways a slave to mere interest. He raised himself again for the battle rather than bow down to those whom he regarded as infinitely beneath him." If he could no longer be conqueror, still less would he hand the reins to his adversaries. He overcame them—but a little more would have vanquished himself in the same stroke.

He persisted then in writing his operas,[2] of which the series spread out until 1741, marking work after work with a growing tendency towards the *opéra-comique* and the style of romances[3] so dear to the

---

[1] *"La Salle"* returned to Paris, where she made her reappearance at the Académie de Musique in August, 1735, in *les Indes galantes* of Rameau. It is quite remarkable that some pages of this work, such as the superb chaconne at the end, have a character quite Handelian.

[2] *Atalanta* (May 12, 1736), *Arminio* (January 12, 1737), *Giustino* (February 16, 1737), *Berenice* (May 18, 1737), *Faramondo* (January 7, 1738), *Serse* (April 15, 1738), *Imeneo* (November 22, 1740), *Deidamia* (January 10, 1741).

[3] Especially in *Serse* and *Deidamia*.

people at the second half of the eighteenth century. But since 1735 he felt more than ever that the true musical drama for him was the oratorio. He returned victoriously with *Alexander's Feast*, which was composed on the *Ode to St. Cecilia*, by Dryden,[1] and given for the first time on February 19, 1736, at the Covent Garden Theatre.

Who would have believed that this work, robust and sane throughout, was written in twenty days, that it was performed in the midst of his business worries, within an ace of ruin, and when he was threatened with that grave malady which was to throw the mind of Handel for evermore into gloom ?

·   ·   ·   ·   ·   ·

For several years trouble pursued him. Work and excessive worry had undermined an iron constitution. He tried the baths at Tunbridge Wells during the summer of 1735, and probably also in 1736, but with no success. He could not sleep. His theatre was always on his mind. He made superhuman efforts to keep it going. From January, 1736, to April, 1737, he directed two seasons of Opera, two seasons of oratorio, and

[1] Dryden the poet wrote this brilliant poem in 1697 in a night of inspiration. Clayton had set it to music in 1711 ; and again about 1720 Benedetto Marcello wrote a cantata in the ancient manner on an Italian adaptation of the English ode by the Abbé Conti. A friend of Handel, Newburgh Hamilton, arranged Dryden's poem with great discretion for Handel's oratorio.

Handel had already written several times in honour of St. Cecilia. Some fragments of four cantatas to St. Cecilia are to be found in Vol. LII of the great Breitkopf edition (*Cantate italiane con stromenti*). They were all written in London, the first about 1713.

composed a song, an oratorio, a Psalm, and four
operas.[1] On April 12, or 13, 1737, the machine
broke down. He was smitten with paralysis, his
right side was attacked, his hand refused all
service, and even his mind was affected. In his
absence his theatre closed its doors, bankrupt.[2]
During the whole of the summer Handel remained
in a pitiful state of depression. He refused to care
for anything ; all hope was lost. Finally, his
friends succeeded in inducing him, towards the end
of August, to try the baths at Aix-la-Chapelle. The
cure had a miraculous effect. In a few days he was
restored. In October he returned to London, and
immediately the refreshed giant resumed the
struggle, writing in three months two operas, and
the magnificent *Funeral Anthem* on the death of
the Queen.[3]

Sad days were in store, however. His creditors
seized him, and he was threatened with imprison-
ment. Happily a sympathetic movement was
inaugurated in favour of the artist so harassed by
his kind. A benefit concert, to which his pride
reluctantly submitted,[4] at the end of March, 1738,

---

[1] *Alexander's Feast* (January, 1736), *Atalanta* (April), *Wedding
Anthem* (April), *Giustino* (August), *Arminio* (September),
Berenice (December).

[2] June 1, 1737. But on June 11 the rival opera also closed
its doors, ruined. Handel, like Samson, dragged down in his
own fall the enemy whom he wished to annihilate.

[3] On November 15, 1737, Handel commenced *Faramondo ;*
from December 7 to 17 he wrote the *Funeral Anthem.* On
December 24 he finished *Faramondo.* On December 25 he
commenced *Serse.*

[4] He said that these kinds of concerts were but a way of
begging.

had an unexpected success. It freed him from the most pressing of his debts. In the following month a token of public admiration was given him. His statue was erected in the Vauxhall Gardens.[1] In the springtime of 1738 he began to feel, with returning strength, confidence in the future. The horizon cleared. He was encouraged by such faithful sympathy. He returned to life, and made his presence felt again.

On July 23 he commenced *Saul*; on August 8 he had written two acts of it; by September 27 the work was finished. On October 7 he began *Israel in Egypt*; by October 28 the work was achieved. Still pushing strenuously forward, on October 4 he launched the first volume of his organ concertos with the publisher Walsh, and on the 7th he took to him his *Seven Trios or Sonatas in two parts, with bass*, Opus 5. For those who know these joyful works, which dominate like two Colossi the two oratorios of victory, this superhuman effort had the effect of a force of Nature, like a field which breaks into flower in a single night of springtime.

Saul is a great epic drama, flowing and powerful, where the humorous and the tragic intermingle. *Israel* is one immense chorale, the most gigantic effort which has ever been made in oratorio, not

[1] Vauxhall was a beautiful garden on the Thames, the meeting place of London Society. Every evening except Sunday from the end of April to the beginning of August, vocal, orchestral, and organ concerts were given. The manager of these entertainments, Tyers, caused a white marble statue of Handel by the sculptor Roubiliac to be placed in a niche of a large grotto. The same sculptor later on executed Handel's statue for his monument in Westminster Abbey.

only with a single but with combined choirs.[1]
The audacious originality of the conception and its
austere grandeur almost stunned the public of his
day. The living Handel breathes throughout the
work.

The hopes which Handel had founded on England
caused him fresh uneasiness. Times were hard.
Since the winter of 1739, theatrical performances, and
even concerts, were suspended for several months
on account of the war, and the extreme cold. Handel,
to keep himself warm, wrote in eight days the little
Ode to St. Cecilia (November 29, 1739) ; in sixteen
days *L'Allegro, Il Penseroso, ed Il Moderato* of
Milton (January–February, 1740) ; in a month the
Concerti Grossi, Opus 6.[2] But the success of these
charming works, graven out with loving care, into
which Handel had perhaps put more than into any
other his own personal feelings, his poetic and
humorous reproductions of nature,[3] was hardly
sufficient yet to establish his affairs, at one time so
embarrassed. Once more, as in the time of *Deborah*
and *Arianna*, he was attacked by a coalition of

[1] In the first part of *Israel in Egypt* there is not a single solo
air to be found. In the whole work there are nineteen choruses
against four solos and three duets. The poem of *Saul* which
Chrysander at first attributed to Jennens appears to have been,
as he discovered later on, the work of Newburgh Hamilton.
For *Israel*, Handel entirely dispensed with a librettist, taking
the pure Bible text.

[2] Written between September 29 and October 30, 1739.
Handel further prepared in November, 1740, the Second Volume
of Organ Concertos (six). The same month he opened his last
season of opera, giving on November 22 *Imeneo*, which was
only played twice, and on January 14, 1741, *Deidamia*, which
was only given three times.

[3] Especially in the *Allegro* and in certain *Concerti Grossi*.

fashionable people. One does not know how Handel had wounded them,[1] but they were resolved on his downfall. They avoided his concerts. They even paid men to pull down his placards in the streets. Handel, tired and disheartened, suddenly threw up the combat.[2] He decided to leave England, where he had lived for nearly thirty years, and where he had increased his fame so much. He announced his last concert for April 8, 1741.[3]

.   .   .   .   .

It is a remarkable thing that often in the lives of the great men, just at the moment when all seems lost, or things are at their lowest ebb, they are nearest to the fulfilment of their destiny. Handel appeared vanquished. Just at that very hour he wrote a work which was destined to establish permanently his immortality.

[1] An anonymous letter published in the *London Daily Post* of April 4, 1741, alludes to a single false step made without premeditation.

[2] In the midst of his misery he still thought of those more miserable than himself. In April, 1738, he founded with other well-known English musicians, Arne, Greene, Pepusch, Carey, etc., the Society of Musicians for the succour of aged and poor musicians. Tormented as he was himself, he was more generous than all the others. On March 20, 1739, he gave *Alexander's Feast* with a new Organ Concerto for the benefit of the Society. On March 28, 1740, he conducted his *Acis and Galatea* and his little *Ode on Cecilia's day*. On March 14, 1741, in his worst days he gave the *Parnasso in festa*, a gala spectacle very onerous for him with five Solo Concertos by the most celebrated instrumentalists. Later on he bequeathed £1000 to the Society.

[3] A clumsy friend tried to raise a public charity in an anonymous letter to the *London Daily Post* (see above). He made excuses for Handel, and thus gave the composer the most cruel blow of all. (The clumsiness of a bear !) This letter is found at the end of Chrysander's third volume.

He left London.[1] The Lord-Lieutenant of Ireland invited him to Dublin to direct some concerts. Thus it was, so he said, "in order to offer this generous and polished nation something new" that he composed *The Messiah* on a poem by his friend Jennens.[2] They had already given many of his religious works in Dublin for charitable concerts.[3] Handel was received enthusiastically. The letter which he wrote on December 29 to Jennens bubbles over with joy. The time which he passed in Dublin was, together with his early years in Italy, the happiest in his life. From December 23, 1741, to April 7, 1742, he gave two series of six concerts, and always with the same success. Finally, on April 12, the first hearing of *The Messiah* took place in Dublin. The proceeds of the concert were devoted to charitable objects, and the success was very considerable.[4]

[1] On November 4, 1741, he still had time to see, before his departure, the reopening of the Italian Opera, under the direction of Galuppi, supported by the English nobility.

[2] Handel wrote the *Messiah* between August 22 and September 14, 1741. Certain historians have attributed the composition of the *libretto* to him. There is no reason for robbing Jennens, a man of intelligence, author of the excellent poem of *Belshazzar*, of this honour, and of that shown by the fact that Handel changed none of the text which Jennens gave him. A letter of March 31, 1745, to a friend (quoted by Schoelcher) shows that Jennens found the music of the *Messiah* hardly worthy of his poem.

[3] The great Musical Society of Dublin, the Philharmonic, gave only benevolent concerts. For Handel they made a special arrangement. It suited them that Handel reserved one concert for charity. Handel was engaged there with gratefulness by promising "some better music." This "better music" was the *Messiah*. See an article on *Music in Dublin from* 1730 *to* 1754 by Dr. W. H. Gratten-Flood, I.M.G. (April–June, 1910).

[4] But not at London, where Handel gave the *Messiah* only three times in 1743, twice in 1745, and not again until 1749. The cabals of the pious tried to stifle it. He was not allowed to

H

Eight days after having finished *The Messiah* (that is to say, before he had yet arrived in Ireland) Handel had commenced *Samson*, which was finished in five weeks, from the end of September to the end of October, 1741. However, he did not give it in Dublin. Doubtless he could not find the interpreters which he desired for this colossal drama, rich in choral scenes and in difficult *rôles*.[1] Perhaps also he reserved the work for the following season in Dublin, when he hoped to return, but the expected invitation which he awaited in London did not come, and it was in London that *Samson* reached its first hearing on February 18, 1743.

To this heroic oratorio, based on the sublime *Samson Agonistes* of Milton,[2] succeeded a light opera, which bore, nevertheless, the name of oratorio, the libretto of which was based on a poem by Congreve : *Semele* (June 3 to July 4, 1743). It afforded a relief for him between these two Herculean works. In the same month in which he finished *Semele*, Handel wrote his monumental

put the title of the oratorio on the bills. It was called A Sacred Oratorio. It was only at the close of 1750 that the victory of the *Messiah* was complete. Handel all his life preserved his connection with charitable objects. He conducted it once a year for the benefit of the Foundling Hospital. Even when he was blind he remained faithful to this noble practice, and in order to better preserve the monopoly of the work for the Hospital he forbade anyone to publish anything from it before his death.

Since then one knows what a number of editions of the *Messiah* have appeared. The Schoelcher collection in the Paris Conservatoire has brought together sixty-six published between 1763–1869.

[1] The character of Delilah is one of the most complex which Handel has created, and the parts of Samson and Harapha require exceptional voices.

[2] Milton's poem had been adapted by Newburgh Hamilton.

Dettingen Te Deum, to celebrate the victory of the
Duke of Cumberland over the French.[1] *Joseph*,
written in August and September of the same year,
on a very touching poem by James Miller, reveals a
sweet yet melancholy fancy, a little insipid, on
which, however, the strong portrait of Simeon
projects itself forcibly.

1744 was one of Handel's most glorious years
from the creative point of view, but one of the most
miserable in outward success. He wrote nearly
simultaneously his two most tragic oratorios, the
great Shakespearian drama of *Belshazzar* (July–
October, 1744), the rich poem of which was furnished
for him by his friend Jennens ;[2] and the sublime
tragedy of the ancient *Hercules*, a musical drama,[3]
which marks the culmination of the Handelian
musical drama, and indeed one might say of the
whole musical theatre before Gluck.

Never was the hostility of the English public
more roused against him. The same hateful cabal
which had already thrice threatened to bring about

[1] The Battle of Dettingen took place on June 27, 1743.
Handel had already finished on July 17 his *Te Deum*, which
was solemnly performed on the following November 27 in Westminster Abbey.

[2] Too slowly for the liking of Handel, who composed it bit by
bit as the acts were sent him. There are five letters from him
to Jennens dated June 9, July 19, August 21, September 13
and October 2, 1744, where he presses him to send at once
the rest of the poem, expressing his own admiration for the
second act, which he said provides new means of expression
and furnishes the opportunity of giving some special ideas,
" finally asking him to cut down the work a little, as it was too
long " (see Schoelcher).

[3] Handel wrote it during the forced pauses in the composition
of *Belshazzar*, and produced it at the commencement of 1745.

his downfall again rose against him. They invited
the fashionable world in London to their *fêtes*,
specially organised on the days when the performances of his oratorios were to have taken place,
with the object of robbing him of his audience.
Bolingbroke and Smollett both speak of the plots
of certain ladies to ruin Handel. Horace Walpole
says that it was the fashion to go to the Italian
Opera when Handel directed his oratorio concerts.
Handel, whose force of energy and genius had
weakened since his first failure of 1735, was involved
afresh in bankruptcy at the beginning of 1745.
His griefs and troubles, and the prodigious expendi-
ture of force which he made, seemed again on the
point of turning his brain. He fell into extreme
bodily prostration and lowness of spirit, similar to
that of 1737, and this lasted for the space of eight
months, from March to October, 1745.[1] By a
miracle he was able to rise out of this abyss, and
by unforeseen events, where music was his only
aid, he became more popular than he ever was
before.

The Pretender, Charles Edward, landed in
Scotland; the country rose up. An army of High-
landers marched on London. The city was in
consternation. A great national movement arose
in England, Handel associated himself with it. On
November 14, 1745, he brought to light at Drury
Lane his *Song made for the Gentlemen Volunteers*

[1] The letters quite recently published throw much light on
this troublous period in Handel's life (William Barclay-Squire:
Handel in 1745, in the H. Riemann Festschrift, 1909, Leipzig).

of the City of London,[1] and he wrote two oratorios,
which were, so to speak, immense national hymns :
the *Occasional Oratorio,*[2] where Handel called the
English to rise up against invasion, and *Judas
Maccabæus*[3] (July 9 to August 11, 1746), the Hymn
of Victory, written after the rout of the rebels at
Culloden Moor, and for the *fête* on the return of the
conqueror, the ferocious Duke of Cumberland, to
whom the poem was dedicated.

These two patriotic oratorios, where Handel's
heart beat with that of England, and of which the
second, *Judas Maccabæus*, has retained even to our
own day its great popularity, thanks to its broad
style and the spirit which animates it,[4] brought

[1] Two examples of the song appear in the Schoelcher Collection at the Paris Conservatoire.

Handel also wrote in July, 1746, for the return of the Duke
of Cumberland, a song on the victory over the rebels by His
Royal Highness the Duke of Cumberland, which was given at
Vauxhall (a copy of this song also appears in the Schoelcher
Collection).

[2] Finished in the early days of December, 1745, and given in
February, 1746. The text was founded partly on the Psalms of
Milton and partly on the Bible. Handel inserted in the third
part several of the finest pages from *Israel in Egypt*. In one of
the solos the principal theme of Rule Britannia which was later
to be composed by Arne appears.

[3] The poem, very mediocre, was by the Rev. Dr. Thomas
Morell, who was the librettist for the last oratorios of Handel.

[4] It was not one of Handel's oratorios, of which the style
was in the popular vein, and where one finds further grand
ensembles and solos closely connected with the Chorus.

Gluck journeyed to London at the end of 1745. He was
then thirty-one years old. He gave two operas in London, *La
Caduta de' Giganti* and *Artamene*. (Certain solos from them are
to be found in the very rare collection of *Delizie dell' opere*, Vol.II,
London,Walsh,possessed by the library of the Paris Conservatoire.)
This journey of Gluck in England has no importance in the
story of Handel, who showed himself somewhat scornful in his
regard for Gluck's music. But it was not so for Gluck, who all his

more fortune to Handel than all the rest of his works together.   After thirty-five years of continuous struggle, plot and counterplot, he had at last obtained a decisive victory.   He became by the force of events *the national musician of England.*

.   .   .   .   .   .

Freed from material cares, which had embittered his life,[1] Handel took up the work of his composition again, with more tranquillity, and in the following years came many of his happiest works.   *Alexander Balus* (June 1 to July 4, 1747)[2] is, like *Semele*, a concert opera, well developed ; the orchestration being exceptionally rich and subtle.   *Joshua* (July 30 to August 18, 1747)[3] is a somewhat pale *replica* of *Judas Maccabæus*.   A gentle love idyll blossoms amidst the pompous choruses.   *Solomon* (June, 1748)[4] is a musical festival, radiating poetry and gladness.   *Susanna* (July 11, 1724, to August,

life professed the most profound respect for Handel.   He regarded him as his master ; he even imagined that he imitated him (see Michael Kelly : *Reminiscences*, I, 255), and certainly one is struck by the analogies between certain pages in Handel's oratorios written from 1744 to 1746 (notably *Hercules* and *Judas Maccabæus*) and the grand operas of Gluck.   We find in the two funeral scenes from the first and second acts of *Judas Maccabæus* the pathetic accents and harmonies of Gluck's *Orpheus*.

[1] After 1747 Handel, abandoning his system of subscriptions, turned his back on his aristocratic clientèle, which had treated him so shamefully, and opened his theatre to all.   It paid him. The middle classes of London responded to his appeal.   After 1748 Handel had full houses at nearly all his concerts.

[2] Poem founded on the book of Maccabees by Thomas Morell.   The first performance March 23, 1748.

[3] Poem by Thomas Morell, first performances March 9, 1748.

[4] The poem, apparently, by Thomas Morell, notwithstanding its want of mention in his notes.   First performance March 17, 1749.

1748), grave and gay by turns, realistic yet lyric, is a hybrid kind of work, but very original.

Finally, in the spring of 1749, which marks, so it seems, the end of Handel's good fortune, he wrote his brilliant Firework Music—a model for popular open-air *fêtes*—produced on April 27, 1749, by a monster orchestra of trumpets, horns, oboes, and bassoons, without stringed instruments, on the occasion of the Firework display given in Green Park to celebrate the Peace of Aix la Chapelle.[1]

More solemn works followed these gay pieces. At this moment of his life the spirit of melancholy raised its grey head before the robust old man, who seemed to be obsessed by the presentiment of some coming ill fortune.

On May 27, 1749, he conducted at the Foundling Hospital[2] for the benefit of waifs and strays, his beautiful *Anthem for the Foundling Hospital*,[3] which was inspired by his great pity for these little

[1] The Firework Music has been published in Volume XLVII of the Complete Handel Edition. For the performance on April 27, 1749, the orchestra numbered one hundred. Schoelcher has published a correspondence on the subject of this work between Lord Montague, General-in-chief of the Artillery, and Charles Frederick, Controller of the King's fireworks. One sees there that very serious differences arose between Handel and Lord Montague.

[2] The Foundling Hospital was founded in 1739 by an old mariner, Thomas Coram, " for the maintainance and education of abandoned children." Handel devoted himself to this institution, and gave performances of the *Messiah* annually for its funds. In 1750 he was elected a Governor of the Hospital, after he had made it a gift of an organ.

[3] Vol. XXXVI of the Complete Handel Edition. The Foundling Anthem, of which more than one page is taken from the Funeral Anthem, finishes with the Hallelujah from the *Messiah* in its original form.

unfortunates. From June 28 to July 31 he wrote
a pure masterpiece, *Theodora*, his most intimate
musical tragedy, his only Christian tragedy besides
The Messiah[1]. From the end of that same year
dates also his music for a scene from Tobias Smollett's *Alceste*, which was never played, and from
which Handel took the essential parts for his *Choice
of Hercules*.[2] A little time after he made his last
voyage to Halle. He arrived on German soil at the
moment when Bach died, July 28, 1750. Indeed he
nearly ended his life there himself in the same week
by a carriage accident.[3]

He recovered quickly, and on January 21, 1751,
when he commenced the score of *Jephtha*, he
appeared to be in robust health, despite his sixty-
six years. He wrote the first act at a stretch in
thirteen days. In eleven days more he had arrived
at the last scene but one of Act II. Here he had to
break off. Already in the preceding pages he only
progressed with difficulty ; his writing, so clear and
firm at the commencement, became sticky, con-
fused, and trembling.[4] He had started on the
final chorus of Act II : " How dark, O Lord, are Thy
Ways." Hardly had he written the opening *Largo*
than he had to stop working. He wrote :

---

[1] The libretto was inspired by the *Théodore vierge et martyre*
of Corneille.

[2] Written between June 28 and July 5, and produced on
March 1, to follow Alexander's feast as " a new act added."

[3] A paragraph in the *General Advertiser* of August 21, 1750,
tells us that Handel was very seriously hurt between La Haye
and Amsterdam, but that he was already out of danger.

[4] The facsimile of the autograph manuscript was published
by Chrysander, for the second centenary of Handel in 1885.

" I reached here on Wednesday, February 13, *had
to discontinue on account of the sight of my left eye."* [1]

The work was broken off for ten days. On February
23 (which was his birthday) he wrote in:

" Feel a little better. Resumed work " ;

and he wrote the music to those foreboding words:

" Grief follows joy as night the day."

He took hardly five days to finish this chorus,
which is really sublime. He stopped then for four
months. [2] On June 18 he resumed the third act. He
was again interrupted in the middle. [3] The last four
airs and the final chorus took more time than a
whole oratorio usually occupied. He did not finish
it until August 30, 1751. His sight was then gone.

.   .   .   .   .   .

After that, all was ended. Handel's eyes were
closed for ever. [4] The sun was blotted out, *" Total
eclipse. . . ."* The world was effaced.

He had never suffered so much as in the first year
of his illness, when he was not yet completely blind.
In 1752 he was unable to play the organ at the
productions of his oratorios, and the public, moved
by sympathy, saw him tremble and blanch in

---

[1] Page 182 of MS.

[2] To occupy himself he directed two performances of the
Messiah for the funds of the Foundling Hospital—on April 18
and May 16, " with an improvisation on the organ." He also
tried the cure at Cheltenham.

[3] Page 244 of MS.

[4] He underwent an operation for cataract, the last time on
November 3, 1752. A newspaper stated in January, 1753 :
" Handel has become completely blind."

listening to the admirable complaint of his blind
Samson. But in 1753, when the evil was incurable,
Handel regained his self-possession. He played the
organ again at the twelve performances of oratorios
which he gave each year in Lent, and he kept up
this custom until his death.

But with his vanished sight he had lost the best
source of his inspiration. This man, who was
neither an intellectual nor a mystic, one who
loved above all things light and nature, beautiful
pictures, and the spectacular view of things, who
lived more through his eyes than most of the
German musicians, was engulfed in deepest night.
From 1752 to 1759 he was overtaken by the semi-
consciousness which precedes death. He only wrote
in 1758 a duet and chorus for *Judas Maccabæus*,
" Zion now her head shall raise," and reviving in
that the happy times of other days he took up a
work of his youth, the *Trionfo del Tempo*,[1] which
he now gave in a new version in March, 1757 : *The
Triumph of Time and Truth*.[2]

On April 6, 1759, he again took the organ at a
production of *The Messiah*. His powers failed him
in the middle of a movement. He soon recovered
himself and improvised (it is said) with his habitual
grandeur. Returned home he took to bed. On
April 11 he added a last codicil to his will,[3] bequeath-

---

[1] Written in 1708 at Rome.

[2] Handel had already regiven the Italian work with some
rearrangements and editions in 1737. Thomas Morell adapted
the poem to English, and extended the two acts into three.

[3] This will was written since 1750. Handel added codicils to
it in August, 1756, March and August, 1757, April, 1759. He

HANDEL'S MONUMENT IN WESTMINSTER ABBEY.
(In the "Poets' Corner.")

To face page 107.]

ing munificently £1000 sterling to the Society for the Maintenance of Poor Musicians, and expressing, with tranquillity, his desire of being buried in Westminster Abbey. He said : " I want to die on Good Friday in the hope of rejoining the good God, my sweet Lord and Saviour, on the day of his Resurrection." His wish was accomplished. On Holy Saturday, April 14, at eight in the morning, the sweet singer of *The Messiah* slept with his Lord.

.   .   .   .   .   .

His glory spread after his death. On April 20 he was interred in Westminster Abbey, as he had requested.[1] The annual performances of his oratorios continued in Lent under the direction of his friend, Christopher Smith. Popular performances of them were soon given. The great festival of his Commemoration celebrated at Westminster Abbey and in the Pantheon, from May 26 to June 5, 1784, for the centenary of his birth,[2] was observed all over Europe. New festivals took place in London in 1785, 1786, 1787, 1790, and 1791. On

nominated his niece, Johanna Friderica Flœrchen, of Gotha, *née* Michaelsen, his sole executor. He made several gifts to his friends—to Christopher Smith, to John Rich, to Jennens, to Newburgh Hamilton, to Thomas Morell, and others. He did not forget any of his numerous servants. He left a fortune of about twenty-five thousand pounds, which he had made entirely in his last ten years ; he possessed also a fine collection of musical instruments and a picture gallery in which were two Rembrandts.

[1] A monument, somewhat mediocre, was erected to him. It was the work of Roubiliac, who had already done the statue of Handel for the Vauxhall Gardens.

[2] They were celebrated in reality a year too soon. Burney devoted a whole book to describing these festivals.

the last occasion more than a thousand executants[1]
took part. Haydn was present, and he said,
through his tears, " He is master of us all."

The English performances attracted the attention
of Germany. Two years after the Commemoration,
Johann Adam Hiller produced *The Messiah* in the
Cathedral Church at Berlin, then at Leipzig, and
then at Breslau. Three years later, in 1789, Mozart
made his arrangements of *The Messiah,* of *Acis and
Galatea,* of the *Ode to St. Cecilia,* and of *Alexander's
Feast.*[2] The first complete edition of Handel was
commenced in 1786. A strong feeling of emulation
made itself felt in Germany to imitate the English
festivals, and to restore choral singing, and to found
the *Singakademien* for the preservation of the
national glories.[3] The rendering of Handel's
oratorios inspired Haydn to write *The Creation.*
Beethoven at the end of his life said of Handel :
" See there is the truth."[4] Poets also vied equally

[1] The number of performers never ceased to increase after
the festivals of 1784, when there were 530 or 540, right up to
the famous festivals in the Sydenham Crystal Palace, when the
number reached 1035 in 1854, 2500 in 1857, and 4000 in 1859.
Remember that during the lifetime of Handel the *Messiah* was
performed by thirty-three players and twenty-three singers.
They manufactured for these gigantic performances some
monster instruments ; a double bassoon (already invented in
1727), a special contrabass, some bass trumpets, drums tuned
an octave lower, etc.

[2] These arrangements, executed for the Baron van Swieten,
are far from being irreproachable, and show that Mozart, despite
the assertions of Rochlitz, had not a deep understanding of
Handel's works. However, he wrote an " Overture in the style
of Handel," and suddenly remembered him when he composed
his *Requiem.*

[3] The first was the Singakademie of Berlin, founded in 1790
by Fasch.

[4] In the *Harmonicon* of January, 1824, one finds Beethoven's

in rendering him homage. Goethe admired him, and Herder devoted a chapter to him in his *Adrastea* of 1802. The wars of Independence gave an access of favour to the oratorio of freedom, to *Judas Maccabæus.*

With romanticism the feeling for the genius of Handel was lost. Berlioz, who, if he had but known him truly, and had found a model for that grand popular style which he sought, never understood him. Of all other musicians, those who approached to the spirit of Handel nearest were Schumann and Liszt,[1] but they were exceptional in the lucidity of their perception, and their generous sympathies. It might be said that Handel's art, distorted by the editions and false renderings—quite as much those in Germany as the ridiculously colossal representations in England—would have been completely lost except for the foundation in 1856 of the Handel Society, which devoted itself to the object of publishing an exact and complete edition of the

opinion (quoted by Percy Robinson) : " Handel is the greatest composer who has ever lived. I should like to kneel at his tomb." And in a letter from Beethoven to an English lady (published in the *Harmonicon* of December, 1825) : " I adore Handel." We know that after the 9th Symphony he had the plan of writing some grand oratorios in the style of Handel.

[1] Schumann wrote to Pohl in 1855, that *Israel in Egypt* was his " ideal of a choral work," and, wishing to write a work called *Luther*, he defined this music thus, of which he found the ideal realized by Handel : " A popular oratorio that both country and town-people can understand. . . . A work of simple inspiration, in which the effect depends entirely on the melody and the rhythm, without contrapuntal artifice."

Liszt, *apropos* of the Anthem *Zadock the Priest*, goes into ecstasies over " the genius of Handel, great as the world itself," and very rightly perceives in the author of the *Allegro* and of *Israel*, a precursor of descriptive music.

works of the master. Gervinus was the promoter and Friedrich Chrysander alone accomplished the task. It did not aim at being a critical edition of his works. His ardent apostle sought simply to revive them in their pristine force.[1] He was seconded by the choral societies of north Germany, particularly by the Berlin *Singakademien*, which from 1830 to 1860 never ceased to perform all the oratorios of Handel. On the contrary, Austria remained a long way behind. In 1873, Brahms conducted the first production of *Saul* in Vienna, but the veritable awakening of Handel's art in Germany only dates back about half a score years. One recognized his grandeur, and did not doubt that he had lived. It was chiefly (so it seems) at the first Handel Festival of Mayence in 1895, where *Hercules* and *Deborah* were given, that his astounding dramatic genius was first truly felt there.

To us in France we still await the full revelation of the living scenes of this great and luminous tragic art, so akin to the aims of Ancient Greece.[2]

[1] See, in Chrysander's work, an article by Emil Krause, in the *Monatshefte für Musikwissenschaft*, 1904.

[2] A Société G. F. Handel was founded in Paris in 1909, under the direction of two conductors full of zeal and intelligence, MM. F. Borrel and F. Raugal. It has already done much to awaken the love of Handel in France by giving the large works hitherto unknown in France, such as *Hercules*, the *Foundling Anthem*, and the model performances of the *Messiah* at the Trocadero.

HIS TECHNIQUE AND WORKS

No great musician is more impossible to include in the limits of one definition, or even of several, than Handel. It is a fact that he reached the complete mastery of his style very early (much earlier than J. S. Bach), although it was never really fixed, and he never devoted himself to any one form of art. It is even difficult to see a conscious and a logical evolution in him. His genius is not of the kind which follows a single path, and forges right ahead until it reaches its object. For his aim is none other than to do well whatever he undertook. All ways are good to him—from his early steps at the crossing of the ways, he dominated the country, and shed his light on all sides, without laying siege to any particular part. He is not one of those who impose on life and art a voluntary idealism, either violent or patient ; nor is he one of those who inscribe in the book of life the formula of their campaign. He is of the kind who drink in the life universal, assimilating it to themselves. His artistic will is mainly objective. His genius adapts itself to a thousand images of passing events, to the nation, to the times in which he lived, even to the fashions of his day. It accommodates itself to the various influences, ignóring all obstacles. It weighs other styles and other thoughts, but such is

the power of assimilation and the prevailing equilibrium of his nature that he never feels submerged
and overweighted by the mass of these strange
elements. Everything is duly absorbed, controlled,
and classified. This immense soul is like the sea
itself, into which all the rivers of the world pour
themselves without troubling its serenity.

The German geniuses have often had this power
of absorbing thoughts and strange forms,[1] but it is
excessively rare to find amongst them the grand
objectivism, and this superior impersonality, which
is, so to speak, the hall-mark of Handel. Their
sentimental lyricism is better fitted to sing songs,
to voice the thoughts of the universe in song, than
to paint the universe in living forms and vital
rhythms. Handel is very different, and approaches
much more nearly than any other in Germany
the genius of the South, the Homeric genius of
which Goethe received the sudden revelation on his
arrival at Naples.[2] This capacious mind looks out
on the whole universe, and on the way the universe
depicts itself, as a picture is reflected in calm and
clear water. He owes much of this objectivism to
Italy, where he spent many years, and the fascination of which never effaced itself from his mind, and
he owes even more to that sturdy England, which
guards its emotions with so tight a rein, and which
eschews those sentimental and effervescing effusions,

---

[1] Lessing, in the Preface to his *Beiträge zur Historie und
Aufnahme des Theaters* (1750), gives as the principal characteristic
of the German, "that he appreciates whatever is good, particularly where he finds it, and when he can turn it to his profit."

[2] See the *Voyage en Italie*, May 18, 1787, letter to Herder.

so often displayed in the pious German art; but that he had all the germs of his art in himself, is already shown in his early works at Hamburg.

From his infancy at Halle, Zachau had trained him not in one style, but in all the styles of the different nations, leading him to understand not only the spirit of each great composer, but to assimilate the styles by writing in various manners. This education, essentially cosmopolitan, was completed by his three tours in Italy, and his sojourn of half a century in England. Above all he never ceased to follow up the lessons learnt at Halle, always appropriating to himself the best from all artists and their works. If he was never in France (it is not absolutely proved), he knew her nevertheless. He was anxious to master their language and musical style. We have proofs of that in his manuscripts,[1] and in the accusations made against him by certain French critics.[2] Wherever he passed, he gathered some musical souvenir, buying and collecting foreign works, copying them, or rather (for he had not the careful patience of J. S. Bach, who scrupulously wrote out in his own hand the entire scores of the French organists and the Italian violinists) copying down in hasty and often inexact expressions any idea which struck him in the course of his reading. This vast collection of European thoughts, which only remains in remnants at the Fitzwilliam Museum at Cambridge, was the

[1] French Songs (MSS. in Fitzwilliam Museum, Cambridge); copies in the Schoelcher Collection, in the library of the Paris Conservatoire.

[2] See the Abbé Prevost: *Le Pour et le Contre*, 1733.

I

reservoir, so to speak, from which his creative
genius continually fed itself. Profoundly German
in race and character, he had become a world
citizen, like his compatriot Leibnitz, whom he had
known at Hanover, a European with a tendency for
the Latin culture. The great Germans at the end
of that century, Goethe and Herder, were never
more free, or more universal, than this great Saxon
in music, saturated as he was with all the artistic
thoughts of the West.

He drew not only from the sources of learned and
refined music—the music of musicians; but also
drank deeply from the founts of popular music—
that of the most simple and rustic folk.[1] He loved
the latter. One finds noted down in his manuscripts
the street cries of London, and he once told a friend
that he received many inspirations for his best airs
from them.[2] Certain of his oratorios, like *L'Allegro
ed Il Penseroso*, are threaded with remembrances
of his walks in the English country, and who can
ignore the *Pifferari* (Italian peasant's pipe) in *The*

[1] These are not traits special to Handel alone. The double
stream—encyclopædic and learned on the one hand, popular or
pseudo-popular on the other—was found in an even greater degree
in London amongst the musicians of Handel's time. In the
circle of the *Academy of Antient Musick* there was quite a mania
of archaic eclectism. One of these members, the composer
Roseingrave, even went to the length of having the walls of
his rooms and all his furniture covered with bars of music,
extracted from the works of Palestrina. At the same period
there was felt all over Europe a reaction of popular taste against
that of the savants. It was the day of the little *lieder* by Bononcini or by Keiser. Handel took sides with neither extravagances,
but chose whatever was alive in both movements.

[2] Letter from Lady Luxborough to the poet Shenstone in
1748—quoted by Chrysander.

Messiah, the Flemish carillon in *Saul,* the joyous popular Italian songs in *Hercules,* and in *Alexander Balus?* Handel was not an artist lost in introspection. He watched all around him, he listened, and observed. Sight was for him a source of inspiration, hardly of less importance than hearing. I do not know any great German musician who has been as much a visual as Handel. Like Hasse and Corelli, he had a veritable passion for beautiful pictures. He hardly ever went out without going to a theatre or to a picture sale. He was a connoisseur, and he made a collection, in which some Rembrandts[1] were found after his death. It has been remarked that his blindness (which should have rendered his hearing still more sensitive, his creative powers translating everything into sonorous dreams) soon paralysed his hearing when its principal source of renewal was withdrawn.

Thus, saturated in all the European music of his time, impregnated with the music of musicians, and the still richer music which flows in all Nature herself, which is specially diffused in the vibrations of light and shade, that song of the rivers, of the forest, of the birds, in which all his works abound, and which have inspired some of his most picturesque pages with a semi-romantic colour,[2] he wrote as one speaks, he composed as one breathes. He

[1] His passion of collecting increased with age and fortune. A letter of 1750 reveals him buying some beautiful pictures, including a fine Rembrandt. It was the year before he was smitten with blindness.

[2] From the " *Hauts tilleuls* " of *Almira* up to the Night Chorus in *Solomon.*

never sketched out on paper in order to prepare his
definite work. He wrote straight off as he improvised, and in truth he seems to have been the
greatest improviser that ever was. Whether ex-
temporising on the organ at the midday services
in St. Paul's Cathedral, or playing the *capriccios*
during the *entr'actes* of his oratorios at Covent
Garden—or improvising on the clavier in the
orchestra at the opera, at Hamburg or in London,
or " when he accompanied the singers in a most
marvellous fashion, adapting himself to their
temperament and virtuosity, without having any
written notes," he astounded the connoisseurs of
his time; and Mattheson, who may hardly be
suspected of any indulgence towards him, proclaimed that he had no equal in this. One can truly
say that " he improvised every minute of his life."
He wrote his music with such an impetuosity of
feeling, and such a wealth of ideas, that his hand
was constantly lagging behind his thoughts, and in
order to keep pace with them at all he had to note
them down in an abbreviated manner.[1] But (and

[1] A study of the MS. of *Jephtha* (published in *facsimile* by
Chrysander) affords an opportunity of noticing Handel's speed
of working at composition. On these very pages one reads
various annotations in Handel's own handwriting. At the end
of the first act, for instance, he writes: " *Geendiget* (finished) 2
February." Again, on the same page one reads: "*Völlig* (complete) 13th August, 1751." There were then two different
workings; one the work of invention, the other a work of
completion. It is easy to distinguish them here on account of
the illness which changed the handwriting of Handel after
February 13, 1751. Thanks to this circumstance, one sees that
with the Choruses he wrote the entire subjects in all the voices
at the opening; then he let first one fall, then another, in
proceeding; he finished hastily with a single voice filled in or
even the bass only.

this seems contradictory) he had at the same time an exquisite sense of form. No German surpassed him in the art of writing beautiful, melodic lines. Mozart and Hasse alone were his equals in this. It was to this love of perfection that we attribute that habit which, despite his fertility of invention, causes him to use time after time, the same phrases (those most important, and dearest to him) each time introducing an imperceptible change, a light stroke of the pencil, which renders them more perfect. The examination of these kinds of musical *eaux-fortes* in their successive states is very instructive for the musician who is interested in plastic beauty.[1] It shows also how certain melodies, once written down, continued to slumber in Handel's mind for many years, until they had penetrated his subconscious nature, were applied at first, by following the chances of his inspiration, to a certain situation, which suited them moderately well. They are, so to speak, in search of a body where they can reincarnate themselves, seeking the true situation, the real sentiment of which they are but the latent expression ; and once having found it, they expand themselves with ease.[2]

Handel worked no less with the music of other composers than with his own. If one had the time to

[1] It was so with the melody : *Dolce amor che mi consola* in *Roderigo*, which became the air : *Ingannata una sol volta* in *Agrippina*—and also with the air : *L'alma mia* from *Agrippina*, which was used again for the *Resurrection*, for *Rinaldo* and for *Joshua*.

[2] The Eastern Dance in *Almira* became the celebrated *Lascia ch'io pianga* in *Rinaldo ;* and a joyful but ordinary melody from *Pastor Fido* was transformed to the touching phrase in the *Funeral Ode :* " Whose ear she heard."

study here what superficial readers have called his
plagiarisms, particularly taking, for example, *Israel
in Egypt*, where the most barefaced of these cases
occur, one would see with what genius and insight
Handel has evoked from the very depths of these
musical phrases, their secret soul, of which the first
creators had not even a presentiment. It needed
his eye, or his ear, to discover in the serenade of
Stradella its Biblical cataclysms. Each read and
heard a work of art as it is, and yet not as it is ; and
one may conclude that it is not always the creator
himself who has the most fertile idea of it. The
example of Handel well proves this. Not only did
he create music, but very often he created that of
others for them. Stradella and Erba were only
for him (however humiliating the comparison)
the flames of fire, and the cracks in the wall,
through which Leonardo saw the living figures.
Handel heard great storms passing through the
gentle quivering of Stradella's guitar.[1]

This evocatory character of Handel's genius
should never be forgotten. He who is satisfied with
listening to this music without *seeing* what it
expresses—who judges this art as a purely formal
art, who does not feel his expressive and suggestive
power, occasionally so far as hallucination, will
never understand it. It is a music which paints

[1] One can examine here in detail the two very characteristic
instrumental interludes from Stradella's *Serenata a 3 con stromenti*
which had the fortune of blossoming out into the formidable
choruses of the Hailstones and the Plague of Flies in *Israel*. I
have made a study of this in an article for the S.I.M. review
(May and July, 1910), under the title of *Les plagiats de Handel*.

emotions, souls, and situations, to see the epochs
and the places, which are the framework of the
emotions, and which tint them with their own
peculiar moral tone. In a word, his is an art
essentially picturesque and dramatic. It is scarcely
twenty to thirty years since the key to it was found
in Germany, thanks to the Handel Musical Festivals.
As Heuss says, concerning a recent performance at
Leipzig, " For a proper comprehension no mäster
more than Handel has greater need öf being performed, and *well* performed. One can study J. S.
Bach at home, and enjoy it even more than at a
good concert, but he who has never heard Handel
well performed can with difficulty imagine what he
really is, for really good performances of Handel
are excessively rare." The intimate sense of his
works was falsified in the century which followed
his death by the English interpretations, strength-
ened further still in Germany by those of Mendels-
sohn, and his numerous following. By the exclusion
of and systematic contempt for all the operas of
Handel, by an elimination of nearly all the dramatic
oratorios, the most powerful and the freshest, by a
narrow choice more and more restrained to the four
or five oratorios, and even here, by giving an
exaggerated supremacy to *The Messiah*, by the
interpretation finally of these works, and notably
of *The Messiah* in a pompous, rigid, and stolid
manner, with an orchestra and choir far too numerous and badly balanced, with singers frightfully
correct and pious, without any feeling or intimacy,
there has been established that tradition which

makes Handel a church musician after the style of
Louis XIV, all decoration—pompous columns, noble
and cold statues, and pictures by Le Brun. It is not
surprising that this has reduced works executed on
such principles, and degraded them to a monumental tiresomeness similar to that which emanates
from the bewigged Alexanders, and the very
conventional Christs of Le Brun.

It is necessary to turn back. Handel was never
a church musician, and he hardly ever wrote for the
church. Apart from his *Psalms* and his *Te Deum*,
composed for the private chapels, and for exceptional events, he only wrote instrumental music
for concerts and for open-air *fêtes*, for operas, and
for those so-called oratorios, which were really
written for the theatre. The first oratorios he
composed were really acted: *Acis and Galatea* in
May, 1732, at the Haymarket Theatre, with scenery,
decoration, and costumes, under the title of *English
Pastoral Opera—Esther*, in February, 1732, at the
Academy of Ancient Music after the manner of the
Grecian tragedy, the chorus being placed behind
the stage and the orchestra. And if Handel resolutely abstained from theatrical representation[1]—
which alone gives the full value to certain scenes,
such as the orgie and the dream of Belshazzar,
expressly conceived for acting—on the other hand
he stood out firmly for having his oratorios at the

---

[1] There is reason to believe that he was not absolutely free
in the matter. In 1732, when the Princess Anne wished to have
Esther represented at the opera the Archbishop (Dr. Gibson)
opposed it, and it was necessary to fall back to giving the work
at a concert.

theatre and not in the church. There were not wanting churches any less than dissenting chapels in which he could give his works, and by not doing so he turned against him the opinion of religious people who considered it sacrilegious to carry pious subjects on to the stage,[1] but he continued to affirm that he did not write compositions for the church, but worked for the theatre—a free theatre.[2]

This briefly dramatic character of Handel's works has been well comprehended by the German historians who have studied him during recent times. Chrysander compares him to Shakespeare,[3] Kretzschmar calls him the reformer of musical drama, Volbach and A. Heuss see in him a dramatic musician, and claim for the performance of his oratorios dramatic singers. Richard Strauss, in his introduction to Berlioz's *Treatise of Orchestration*, opposes the great polyphonic and symphonic stream issuing from J. S. Bach with that homophonic and dramatic one which comes from Handel. We hope that the readers of this little book have found here in nearly all these pages a confirmation of these ideas.

· · · · · ·

[1] An anonymous letter published in the *London Daily Post* in April, 1739, dealing with *Israel in Egypt*, defends Handel against the opposition of the bigots, who were then very bitter. The writer protests " that the performance at which he was present was the noblest manner of honouring God . . . it is not the house which sanctifies the prayer, but the prayer which sanctifies the house."

[2] Is not even *Joseph* entitled " a sacred Drama," and *Hercules* " a musical Drama " ?

[3] At the end of his second volume of the Life of Handel.

It remains for us, after having attempted to indicate the general characteristics of Handel's art, to sketch the technique of the different styles in which he worked.

To speak truly, it is difficult to speak of the opera or of the oratorio of Handel. It is necessary to say : *of the operas or of the oratorios,* for we do not find that they point back to any single type. We can verify here what we said at the commencement of this chapter, about the magnificent vitality of Handel in choosing amongst his art forms the different directions of the music of his times.

All the European tendencies at that time are reflected in his operas : the model of Keiser in his early works, the Venetian model in his *Agrippina,* the model of Scarlatti and Steffani in his first early operas ; in the London works he soon introduces English influences, particularly in the rhythms. Then it was Bononcini whom he rivalled. Again, those great attempts of genius to create a new musical drama, *Giulio Cesare, Tamerlano, Orlando ;* later on, those charming ballet-operas inspired by France, *Ariodante, Alcina ;* later still, those operas which point towards the *opéra comique* and the light style of the second half of the century, *Serse Deidamia. . . .* Handel continued to try every other style, without making any permanent choice as did Gluck, with whom alone he can be compared.

Without doubt (and it is his greatest fault in the theatre) he was constrained by the conventions of the Italian Opera at times and by the composition of his troupe of singers to overlook his choruses, and to write operas for solo voices, of which the principal *rôles* were cast for the Prima Donna and for the contralto,[1] but whenever he could, he wrote his operas with choruses, like *Ariodante, Alcina,* and he only owed it to himself that he did not give to the tenor or to the bass their place in the concert of voices.[2] If it was not possible to break the uniformity of the solo voices by the addition of

[1] See the vocal distribution of some of the London Operas :
Radamisto (1720) : 4 Sopranos (of which 3 parts are male characters), 1 Alto, 1 Tenor, 1 Bass.
Floridante (1722) : 2 Sopranos, 2 Contraltos, 2 Basses.
Giulio Cesare (1724): 2 Sopranos, 2 Altos, 1 Contralto (Cæsar's *rôle*), 2 Basses.
Tamerlano (1724) : 2 Sopranos, 1 Contralto (male *rôle*), 1 Alto (Tamerlano), 1 Tenor, 1 Bass.
Admeto (1727) : 2 Sopranos, 2 Altos, 1 Contralto (Admeto), 2 Basses.
Orlando (1732) : 2 Sopranos, 1 Alto (Medora), 1 Contralto (Orlando), 1 Bass.
Deidamia (1747) : 3 Sopranos (one is Achilles' *rôle*), 1 Contralto (Ulysses), 2 Basses.
It is the same in the Oratorios, where one finds such a work as *Joseph* (1744) written for 2 Sopranos, 2 Altos, 1 Contralto (Joseph), 2 Tenors, and 2 Basses.
Thus, without speaking of the shocking inconsistencies of the parts thus travestied, the balance of voices tends to fall off as we go from high to low.

[2] In 1729 he went to Italy to find an heroic tenor, Pio Fabri ; unfortunately he could not secure him for two years.—*Acis and Galatea* (1720) is written for 2 Tenors, 1 Soprano, and 1 Bass.—The most tragic *rôle* in *Tamerlano* (1724) (that of Bajazet) was written for the Tenor, Borosini.—*Rodelinda, Scipione, Alessandro,* all contain Tenor *rôles*.—On the other hand, Handel was not satisfied with having in his theatre the most celebrated basses of the century, the famous Boschi and Montagnana, for whom he wrote such fine *rôles,* such as that of Zoroaster in *Orlando,* and Polyphemus in *Acis and Galatea ;* but he aimed at having several important *rôles* all taken by Basses in the same Opera. In his first version of *Athaliah* (1733) he had written a duet for Basses for Joad and Mathan. But the defection of Montagnana obliged him to give up this idea, which he could only realise in *Israel in Egypt.*

choruses, still he enlivened these solos by the
flexibility and the variety of his instrumental
accompaniments. Such of his most celebrated airs,
as the Garden scene in *Rinaldo*, "*Augelletti che
cantate*," are only in truth an orchestral tone picture.
The voice mingles itself only as an instrument,[1] and
with what art Handel always decides his melodies in
disengaging the beautiful lines, drawing all the parts
possible in pure tone colours from single instruments, and from the voice isolated,—then united,—
and what of his silences !

The appeal of his melodies is much more varied
than one usually believes. If the *Da Capo* form
abounds in his works,[2] it is necessary to admit that
it was practically the only one of that period. In
Almira, Handel uses the form of a little strophic
song, very happily. For this, Keiser supplied him
with models, and he never renounces the use of
these little melodies, so simple and touching, almost
bare, which speak direct to the soul. He seems to
return to them even with special predilection in his
last operas, *Atalanta*, *Giustina*, *Serse*, *Deidamia*.[3]
He gives also to Hasse and to Graun the model of
his six cavatinas, airs in two parts,[4] which they
later on brought into prominence. We find his

---

[1] See also *Giulio Cesare*, *Atalanta*, or *Orlando*.

[2] Especially in certain concert operas, such as *Alcina* (1735),
and also in the last work of Handel, in which one feels his final
torpor, *The Triumph of Time*.

[3] See those Oratorios in which he is not afraid, when necessary,
of introducing little popular songs, as that of the little waiting-
maid in *Susanna* (1749).

[4] See the air of Medea at the beginning of the second act of
Teseo ; Dolce riposo. See also *Ariodante* and *Hercules*.

dramatic airs also have the second part and the repeat.[1]

Even in the *Da Capo*, however, he gives us a variety of forms! Not only does Handel use all styles, but how well does he blend the voices with the instruments in those airs of great brilliance and free virtuosity![2] With what predilection does he ply all these beautiful and learned contrapuntal tissues, as in the *Cara sposa* from *Rinaldo* or the *Ombra cara* from *Radamisto;* but he ever seeks new combinations for the old form. He was one of the first to adopt the little Airs *da capo*, which with Bononcini seems to have been so much the fashion at the commencement of the eighteenth century, and of which *Agrippina* and *Ottone* furnish such delightful examples.[3] To the second part of the air he gave a different character and movement from that of the first part.[4] Still further, in either of the

---

[1] Such as the air at the opening of *Radamisto; Sommi Dei.*— I will mention also the airs written over a Ground-Bass accompaniment without *Da Capo*, of which the most beautiful type is the *Spirito amato* of Cleofide, in *Poro*.

[2] For example the air, *Per dar pregio*, in *Roderigo*. The oboe plays a great part in these musical jousts. Such an air as that in *Teseo* is like a little Concerto for Oboe.

[3] They are extremely short. Some are popular songs. Others in *Agrippina* have just a phrase. Many of these *arietti da capo*, in *Teseo*, in *Ottone*, make one think of those in Gluck's *Iphigénie en Aulide*.

[4] In *Rinaldo*, the air, *Ah crudel il pianto mio*, the first part is a sorrowful *largo*, the second a furious *presto*.—The finest example of this freedom is the air of Timotheus at the beginning of the second act of *Alexander's Feast*. The two parts in this air differ not only by the movements but by the instrumental colouring, by the harmonic character, and by the very essence of the thought; they are two different poems which are joined together, but each being complete in itself.

parts several movements were combined.[1] Sometimes the second part was recitative,[2] or it was
extremely condensed.[3] When Handel had choruses
at his disposal in his oratorios, he often entrusted
the *Da Capo* to the Chorus.[4] He went further : in
Samson, after Micah has sung in the second act the
first two parts of the air " Return, O God of Hosts,"
the chorus takes up the second part at the same
time as Micah returns to the first part. Finally
he attempts to divide the *Da Capo* between two
characters, thus in the second act of *Saul*, Jonathan's
solo "Sin not, O King, against the youth," is followed by Saul's solo, then appearing note for note.

But the most glorious feat of Handel in vocal solos
is the "recitative scene."

It was Keiser who taught him the art of those
moving *recitative-ariosi* with orchestra, which he
had already used in *Almira*, and of which, later on,
J. S. Bach was to take from him the style. He
never ceased to employ it in his London operas, and
he gave the form a superb amplitude. They are not
merely isolated recitatives or preambles to an
extended solo.[5] The story of Cæsar in the third act

---

[1] Examples ; *Teseo*, Medea's ; *Moriro, ma vendicata ; Amadigi*
air, *T'amai quant' il mio cor*.

[2] *Riccardo I*, air, *Morte, vieni*.

[3] In the airs *da capo* of *Ariodante*, the second part is restricted to five bars.

[4] *L'Allegro ed Penseroso*, 1st air, Part 3, *Come with native
lustre shine ;* after the 2nd part comes a recitative, then the chorus
sings the *Da Capo*.—In *Alexander's Feast* the air, *He sung Darius,
great and good ;* after the 2nd part comes a recitative, then the
Da Capo with Chorus, but altogether free ; to speak truly, the
Da Capo is only in the instrumental accompaniment.

[5] Handel has found a musical language passing by imperceptible steps from *recitativo secco*, almost spoken, to *recitativo*

of *Giulio Cesare, Dall' ondoso periglio* is one large musical picture, which expresses in its frame a symphonic prelude, a recitative, the two first parts of an air over the symphonic accompaniment of the opening, a second recitative, then the *Da Capo*. The scene of Bajazet's death in the last act of *Tamerlano* is composed of a series of recitatives with orchestra, and of airs joined together, and passes through all the nuances of feeling, forming from one stage to the other a veritable ladder of life. The scene of Admetes' agony at the opening of the opera of the same name equals in profundity, emotion, and dramatic liberty, the finest recitative scenes of Gluck. The " mad scene " in *Orlando*,[1] and that of Dejanira's despair in the third act of *Hercules*, surpasses them in boldness of realism, and frenetic passion. In the first, burlesque and tragic elements commingle with a truly Shakespearean art. The second is a mighty foaming river, raging with fury and grief. Neither of these two scenes have any analogy in the whole of the musical theatre of the eighteenth century. And *Teseo, Rodelinda, Alessandro, Alcina, Semele, Joseph,*

---

accompagnato, then to the air. In *Scipione* (1726) the phrases of the accompanied *recitative* are enshrined in small frameworks of spoken *recitative* (see p. 23 of the Complete Handel Edition, the air, *Oh sventurati*). The final air in the first act is a compromise between speech and song. The accompanied *recitative* runs naturally into the air.

[1] In the chain of Recitatives and Airs of all kinds which succeed or mingle themselves with it, with an astonishing freedom reflecting one after another, or even at the same time the contradictory ideas which course through Roland's mind, Handel does not hesitate to use unusual rhythms, as the 5–8 here which gives a stronger impression of the hero's madness.

Alexander Balus, Jephtha, all present recitative scenes, or combinations in the same scene of recitatives and very free airs, with instrumental interludes, no less original. Finally a sort of presentiment of the *leit-motiv,* and its psychological employment in *Belshazzar,* should be noticed, where certain instrumental phrases and recitatives seem attached to the character of Nitocris.[1]

. . . . .

The study of Handel's recitatives and airs raises perhaps the greatest problem of artistic interpretation—that of vocal ornamentation.

We know that Handelian singers used to decorate his melodies with graces and melismatic figures, and cadenzas (often very considerable) which have disappeared for the greater part. Chrysander, in

---

[1] It is necessary to consider to some extent the *Arias buffi.* Some have denied Handel the gift of humour. They cannot know him well. He is full of humour, and often expresses it in his works. In his first opera, *Almira,* the *rôle* of Tabarco is in the comic style of Keiser and of Telemann. It is the same feeling which gives certain traits a little *caricaturesque* to the *rôle* of St. Peter in the *Passion after Brockes.* The Polyphemus in *Acis and Galatea* has a fine amplitude of rough buffoonery. But in *Agrippina* Handel derived his subtle irony from Italy ; and the light style with its minute touches and its jerky rhythms from Vinci and Pergolesi (to the letter) appear with Handel in *Teseo* (1713). *Radamisto, Rodelinda, Alessandro, Tolomeo, Partenope, Orlando, Atalanta* afford numerous examples. The scene where Alexander and Roxane are asleep (or pretend to be) is a little scene of musical comedy. *Serse* and *Deidamia* are like tragicomedies, the action of which points to *opéra comique.* But his gift of humour takes another turn in his oratorios, where Handel not only creates complex and colossal types, such as *Delilah* or *Haraphah* in *Samson,* or as the two old men in *Susanna,* but where his Olympian laugh breaks out in the choruses of *L'Allegro,* shaking the sides of the audience with irresistible laughter.

editing Handel's works, found them given as alternatives, and either suppressed them (those which were false to the historic sense of the text) or else rewrote them himself. It was in this last point that he stopped short of all possible guarantees of exactness, or at least of true resemblance. But his revisions found few supporters, and a discussion on his treatment of this subject has been recently raised amongst German musical writers.[1] This debate, the examination of which cannot be entered into in this volume, authorised, it seems, the following conclusions :

(1) The vocal ornaments were not improvised and left to the fancy of the singer, as is often asserted, but they were marked with precise indications in the singer's parts, and also in the score of the accompanying clavecinist :[2]

(2) They were not mere caprices of empty virtuosity, but the result of a reflective virtuosity, and subject to the general style of the piece. They served to accentuate more

[1] See especially Hugo Goldschmidt : *Treatise on Vocal Ornaments*, Volume I, 1907 ; Max Seiffert : *Die Verzierung der Sologesänge in Haendels Messias* (I.M.G., July–September, 1907, and Monthly Bulletin of I.M.G., February, 1908) ; Rudolf Wustmann : *Zwei Messias-probleme* (Monthly Bulletin I.M.G., January, February, 1908).

[2] M. Seiffert has given a description of the whole series of copies of Handel Operas and Oratorios in the Lennard collection of the Fitzwilliam Museum at Cambridge. There are to be found there (in pencil) the indication of the ornaments and vocalises executed by the singers. According to M. Seiffert these indications were by Christopher Smith, the friend and factotum of Handel. According to Mr. Goldschmidt they were put in at the end of the eighteenth century. In any case they show a vocal tradition which affords a good opportunity of preserving for us the physiognomy of the musical ornaments of Handel's time.

K

deeply the expression of the principal melodic lines.[1]

Yet what would be the advantage of restoring these ornaments? Our taste has changed since then, and a stricter reverence forbids us to risk tampering with works of the past by following slavishly such details of tradition and habit which have become meaningless and old-fashioned. Is it better to impose on the public of to-day the older works with all their marks of age improved away by the learning of later generations—or to adapt them soberly in the manner of true feeling, so as to enable them to continue to exercise on us their elevating power? Both sides have been well supported.[2] For myself I consider the first proposition bears on the publication of the scores, and the second on the musical renderings. The mind ought to seek and find out exactly what used to be the case, but when this is done the living are justified in claiming their rights, and by being allowed to reject ancient usages, only preserving such as render these works of genius truly vital.

.   .   .   .   .   .

The vocal ensemble pieces hold a much humbler place in Italian Opera, and Handel has made fewer innovations on this ground than in the vocal solo. However, one finds some very interesting experiments here. His duets are often written in an

[1] This is especially true of the oratorios. In the operas, the ornamentation was much more elaborate and more irrelevant to the expression.

[2] The first, by Mr. Seiffert; the second, by Mr. Goldschmidt.

imitative style, serious and rather sad, in the old Italian school of Provenzale and Steffani,[1] or in the Lully style, where the two voices mingle together note by note with exactitude.[2] But *Atalanta* and *Poro* furnish us also with duets of an alluring freedom and uncommon artistry. And in the duet in the third act of *Orlando*, Handel attempts to differentiate the characters of the weeping Angelica and the furious Roland.—Similarly with the trios written in the strict style of imitation, like that in *Alcina*, Act III, the trio in *Acis and Galatea* carefully defines the couple of lovers from the colossal figure of Polyphemus, the trio in *Tamerlano* contrasts the exasperated Tamerlano with Bajazet and with Asteria, who aggravated him, and the trio in the judgment of Solomon distinguishes the three diverse characters: the calm power of Solomon, the aggressive cries of the wicked mother, and the sorrowful supplications of the good mother. The trio from *Susanna* is no less free, but in the humorous style : one of the two old men madrigalises whilst the other menaces. The *ensemble* forms altogether a most vivid little scene which Mozart himself would not have disowned.[3] Quartets are rare. There are two little ones in the *Triumph of*

[1] *Teseo*, duet, *Addio, mio caro bene ; Esther*, duet by Esther and Ahasuerus: " Who calls my parting soul ? "

[2] *Arminio* (1737), duet from Act III. It is to be noticed that *Arminio* opens also with a duet, a very exceptional thing.

Other duets are in the Sicilian style, as, for instance, that in *Giulio Cesare*, or in the popular English style of the hornpipe, as that of Teofane and Otho in *Ottone ; A' teneri affetti*.

[3] There are to be found also some fine trios in a serious yet virile style in the *Passion according to Brockes* (trio of the believing souls : *O Donnerwort !*) and in the *Chandos Anthems.*

Time, written in Rome. In *Radamisto* Handel made the attempt at a dramatic quartet, but rather clumsily, and with repeated *Da Capo*.[1] The most moving quartet is found in the second act of *Jephtha*. It is in *Jephtha* also, Act III, where the only quintet which he wrote is to be found.

The choruses in the Italian opera of the eighteenth century[2] were reduced to a rudimentary stage, and they consist merely of the union of the voices of soloists at the end of a piece, with certain banal and brilliant acclamations during the course of the action. Notwithstanding this, Handel wrote some stronger ones in *Alcina ;* those of *Giulio Cesare, Ariodante*, and *Atalanta*, were also exceptional in the operas of his time. So with the final choruses Handel arranged after a fashion to escape from the current banality : that of *Tamerlano* is written in a melancholy dramatic vein ; that of *Orlando* strives to preserve the individual character of their personality ; that of *Giulio Cesare* is tacked on to a duet. There are also choruses of people ; the Matelots in *Giustino ;* that of the hunters in *Deidamia*, where the choruses take up the refrain from the air announced by the solo voice. It is the same in *Alessandro*, where the soldiers' chorus repeats Alessandro's hymn, slightly curtailed.

Finally, Handel frequently attempted to build up great musical architecture, raising it by succes-

---

[1] See also the quartet in Act I of *Semele*.
[2] With the exception of the Italian operas played at Venice, in which (thanks to Fux) the tradition of vocal polyphony is maintained—a tradition to be put to such good use later by Hasse and especially Jommelli.

sive stages from solos to ensemble pieces, and then to choruses. At the end of the first act of *Ariodante*, a duet (gavotte style) is taken up by the chorus, then danced without voices ; finally sung and danced. The close of Act III from the same opera gives us a chain of processions, dances, and choruses. The final scenes of *Alessandro* constitute a veritable opera *finale*, 2 duets and a trio running into a chorus.

But it is in his oratorios that Handel attempted these ensemble vocal combinations on the larger scale, and principally that mixture of movements where the powerful contrasts of soli and chorus are grouped together in the same picture.

One sees what a variety of forms and styles he used. Handel was too universal and too objective to believe that one kind of art only was the true one. He believed in two kinds of music only, the good and the bad. Apart from that he appreciated all styles. Thus he has left masterpieces in every style, but he did not open any new way in opera for the simple reason that he went a long way in nearly all paths already opened up. Constantly he experimented, invented, and always with his singularly sure touch. He seemed to have an extraordinary penetrating knowledge in invention, and consequently few artistic regions remained for him to conquer. He made as masterly a use of the recitative as Gluck, or of the *arioso* as Mozart, writing the acts of *Tamerlano*, which are the closest and most heartrending dramas, in the manner of *Iphigénie en Tauride*, the most moving and passionate scenes in music such as certain pages of *Admeto* and *Orlando*, where the humorous and tragic are intermingled in the manner of *Don Giovanni*. He has experimented very happily here in new rhythms.[1] There were new forms, the dramatic duet or quartet, the descriptive symphony opening the opera,[2] refined orchestration,[3] choruses and dances.[4] Nothing seems to have obsessed him. In the following opera we find him returning to the ordinary forms of the Italian or German opera of his time.

. . . . . .

Still less can we say that he held to a rigid form with his operas, which were continually adapted to the changing tastes of the theatre public of his age, and of the singers which he had at his disposal, but when he left the opera for the oratorio he varied no less. It was a perpetual experiment of new forms in the vast framework of the free theatre (*theatre en liberté*) of the concert drama ; and the sort of instinctive ebb and flow in creation seems to have caused his works to succeed one another in groups of analogous or related compositions, each work in a nearly opposite style of feeling and form. In each one Handel indulged momentarily in a certain side of his feelings, and when that was finished he found himself in the possession of other feelings which had been accumulating whilst he was drawing on his first. He thus kept up a perpetual

[1] The 5–8 time in *Orlando* ; the 9–8 in *Berenice*.
[2] The Introduction to *Riccardo I* represents a vessel wrecked in a tempestuous sea.
[3] *Giulio Cesare :* Scene on Parnassus.
[4] *Ariodante, Alcina.*

balance, which is like the pulsation of life itself.
After the realistic *Saul* comes the impersonal epic of
Israel in Egypt. After this colossal monument
appear the two little *genre* pictures, *The Ode to
Cecilia* and *L'Allegro ed Penseroso*. After the
Herculean *Samson*, an heroic and popular tragic
comedy sprang forth, the charming flower of *Semele*,
an opera of romanticism and gallantry.

But if the oratorios are so wonderfully varied
they have one characteristic in common even more
than the operas, they are musical dramas. It was
not that religious thought turned Handel to this
choice of Biblical subjects, but as Kretzschmar has
well shown, it was on account of the stories of the
Bible heroes being a part of the very life-blood of
the people whom he addressed. They were known
to all, whilst the ancient romantic stories could only
interest a society of refined and spoilt *dilettanti*.
Without doubt, these oratorios were not made for
representation, did not seek scenic effects, with
rare exceptions, as for instance the scene of the orgy
of *Belshazzar*, where one feels that Handel had
drawn on the direct vision of theatrical representation, but passions, spirits, and personalities were
represented always in a dramatic fashion. Handel
is a great painter of characters, and the Delilah in
Samson, the Nitocris in *Belshazzar*, the Cleopatra
in *Alexander Balus*, the mother in *Solomon*, the
Dejanira in *Hercules*, the beautiful Theodora, all
bear witness to the suppleness and the profundity
of his psychological genius. If in the course of the
action, and the depicting of the ordinary sentiments,

he abandoned himself freely to the flow of pure music, in the moments of passionate crises he is the equal of the greatest masters in musical drama. Is it necessary to mention the terrible scenes in the third act of *Hercules*, the beautiful scenes of *Alexander Balus*, the Dream of *Belshazzar*, the scenes of *Juno* and the death of *Semele*, the recognition of Joseph and his brothers, the destruction of the temple in *Samson*, the second act of *Jephtha*, the prison scenes in *Theodora*, or in the first act of *Saul*, and dominating all, like great pictures, certain of the choruses in *Israel in Egypt*, in *Esther*, and in *Joshua*, and in the *Chandos Anthems*, which seem veritable tempests of passion, great upheavals of overpowering effect? It is by these choruses that the oratorio is essentially distinguished from the opera. It is in the first place a choral tragedy. These choruses, which are nearly eliminated in Italian Opera during the time of the Barberini, held a very important place in French Opera, but their *rôle* was limited to that of commentator or else merely decorative. In the oratorio of Handel they became the very life and soul of the work. Sometimes they took the part of the ancient classical chorus, which exposed the thought of the drama when the hidden fates led on the heroes to their destinies—as in *Saul, Hercules, Alexander Balus, Susanna.* Sometimes they added to the shock of human passions the powerful appeal of religion, and crowned the human drama with a supernatural aureole, as in *Theodora* and *Jephtha*. Or finally they became the actual actors themselves, or the enemy-people and the God who guided them. It is remarkable that in his very first oratorio *Esther*, Handel had this stroke of genius. In the choruses there we see the drama of an oppressed people and their God who led them by his voice suberbly depicted. In *Deborah* and *Athaliah* also, two nations are in evidence. In *Belshazzar* there are three, but in his chief work of this kind, *Israel in Egypt*, the greatest choral epic which exists, is entirely occupied by Jehovah and His people.

The choruses are in the most diverse styles. Some are in the church style, and a little antiquated;[1] others tend towards the opera—even the *opéra bouffe*;[2] some exhale the perfume of the madrigals at the end of the sixteenth century,[3] and the Academy of Ancient Music in London sought to sustain this art in honour. On the other hand, Handel has frequently used them in the form of a chorale, simple or varied,[4] above all, he employs the choral double fugue in a most astounding manner,[5] and he carries everything on with that impetuosity of genius which drew to him the admiration of the sternest critics of his time, such as Mattheson. His instinct as a great constructor loved to alternate homophonic music with fugal choruses,[6] the massive columns of musical harmony with the moving contrapuntal in superimposed strata, very cleverly

[1] See *Israel in Egypt*.
[2] *Belshazzar, Susanna, L'Allegro, Samson.*
[3] *Saul, Theodora, Athalia.*
[4] *Passion according to Brockes, Chandos Anthems, Funeral Anthem, Foundling Anthem.*
[5] *Anthems, Jubilate, Israel in Egypt.*
[6] *Israel in Egypt, Messiah, Belshazzar, Chandos Anthems.*

framing his dramatic choruses in a most imposing architecture of decorative and impersonal character. His choruses are sometimes tragic scenes,[1] or comedy (see the *Vaudeville*),[2] sometimes *genre* pictures.[3] Handel knew most admirably how to weave in popular motives,[4] or to mingle the dance with the song.[5]

But what belongs chiefly to him—not that he invented it, but made the happiest use of it—is the musical architecture of solo and chorus alternating and intermingled. Purcell and the French composers had given him this idea. He attempted it in his earliest religious works, especially in his *Birthday Ode for Queen Anne*, 1713, where nearly every solo air is taken up again by the following chorus.[6] He had a great feeling for light and pleased himself by introducing in the middle of his choral masses, solo songs which soared up into the air like birds.[7] His dramatic genius knew, when required, how to draw from this combination the most astounding effects. Thus in the *Passion after Brockes*, 1716, where the dialogue of the Daughter of Sion and the chorus *Eilt ihr angefochten Seelen*, with its questions, its responses, its Æschylian interjections, served as

---

[1] *Samson, Saul, Israel in Egypt.*

[2] *L'Allegro, Susanna, Belshazzar, Alexander Balus.*

[3] *Solomon, L'Allegro.*

[4] *Hercules, Saul, Semele, Alexander Balus, Solomon.*

[5] I have noticed above the Chorus-Dances in *Giulio Cesare, Orlando, Ariodante, Alcina.* There are also veritable choral dances in *Hercules, Belshazzar, Solomon, Saul* (the Bell scene), *Joshua* (Sacred dance in Act II over a Ground-Bass).

[6] So in *Athalia, Alexander's Feast, L'Allegro, Samson* (Michel's rôle).

[7] *Jubilate, Funeral Anthem.*

Bach's model for his St. Matthew Passion. At the end of *Israel in Egypt*, after those great choral mountains of sounds, by an ingenious contrast a female voice is heard alone without accompaniment, and then a hymn alternating with the chorus which repeats it. It is the same again at the end of the little short *Ode to St. Cecilia.·*

In the *Occasional Oratorio* a duet for Soprano and Alto alternates with the choruses, but it is in *Judas Maccabæus* where he best achieves this combination of solos and the chorus. In this victorious epic of an invaded people, who rose up and overcame their oppressors, the individualities are scarcely distinguished from the heroic soul of the nation, and the chiefs of the people are only the choralists, whose songs set dancing the enormous ensembles which unfold themselves in powerful and irresistible progressions, like a giant's procession up a triumphal staircase.

It follows then that when the orchestra is added to the dialogue of solos and of choruses, the third element enters into the psychological drama, sometimes in apparent opposition to the two others. Thus in the second act of *Judas Maccabæus* the orchestra which sounds the battle calls makes a vivid contrast to the somewhat funereal choruses on which they are interposed: *We hear the pleasing dreadful call,* or to put it better, they complete them, and fill in the picture. After Death—Glory.

The oratorio being a " free theatre," it becomes necessary for the music to supply the place of the scenery. Thus its picturesque and descriptive *rôle* is strongly developed and it is by this above all that Handel's genius so struck the English public. Camille Saint-Saens wrote in an interesting letter to C. Bellaigue,[1] " I have come to the conclusion that it is the picturesque and descriptive side, until then novel and unreached, whereby Handel achieved the astonishing favour which he enjoyed. This masterly way of writing choruses, of treating the fugue, had been done by others. What really counts with him is the colour—that modern element which we no longer hear in him. . . . He knew nothing of exotism. But look at *Alexander's Feast, Israel in Egypt*, and especially *L'Allegro ed Penseroso*, and try to forget all that has been done since. You find at every turn a striving for the picturesque, for an effect of imitation. It is real and very intense for the medium in which it is produced, and it seems to have been unknown hitherto."

Perhaps Saint-Saens lays too much weight on the " masterly way of writing his choruses," which was not so common in England, even with Purcell. Perhaps he accentuates too much also the real influence of the French in matters of picturesque and descriptive music and the influence which it exerted on Handel.[2] Finally, it is not necessary to represent these descriptive tendencies of Handel as exceptional in his time. A great breath of nature

[1] Quoted by M. Bellaigue in *Les Époques de la Musique*, Vol. I, page 109.

[2] In the time of Lully and his school, the French were the leaders in musical painting, especially for the storms. Addison made fun of it, and the parodies of the *Théâtre de la Foire* often amused people by reproducing in caricature the storms of the *Opéra*.

passed over German music, and pushed it towards tone-painting. Telemann was, even more than Handel, a painter in music, and was more celebrated than Handel for his realistic effects. But the England of the eighteenth century had remained very conservative in music, and had devoted itself to cultivating the masters of the past. Handel's art was then more striking to them on account of " its colour " and " its imitative effects." I will not say with Saint-Saens that " there was no question of exotism with him," for Handel seems to have sought this very thing more than once ; notably in the orchestration of certain scenes for the two Cleopatras, of *Giulio Cesare*, and of *Alexander Balus*. But that which was constantly with him was tone-painting, the reproduction through passages of music of natural impressions, a painting very characterised, and, as Beethoven put it, " more an expression of feelings than of painting," a poetic evocation of the raging tempests, of the tranquillity of the sea, of the dark shades of night, of the twilight which envelops the English country, of the parks by moonlight, of the sunrise in springtime, and of the awakening of birds. *Acis and Galatea, Israel in Egypt, Allegro, The Messiah, Semele, Joseph, Solomon, Susanna*, all offer a wondrous picture gallery of nature, carefully noted by Handel with the sure stroke of a Flemish painter, and of a romantic poet at the same time. This romanticism struck powerfully on his time with a strength which would not be denied. It drew upon him both admiration and violent criticism. A letter of 1751 depicts him as a Berlioz or Wagner, raising storms by his orchestra and chorus.

" He cannot give people pleasure after the proper fashion," writes this anonymous author in his letter, " and his evil genius will not allow him to do this. He imagines a new *grandioso* kind of music, and in order to make more noise he has it executed by the greatest number of voices and instruments which one has ever heard before in a theatre. He thinks thus to rival not only the god of musicians, but even all the other gods, like Iöle, Neptune, and Jupiter : for either I expected that the house would be brought down by his tempest, or that the sea would engulf the whole. But more unbearable still was his thunder. Never have such terrible rumblings fallen on my head."[1]

Similarly Goethe, irritated and upset, said, after having heard the first movement of the Beethoven C Minor symphony, " It is meaningless. One expected the house to fall about one's ears."

It is not by chance that I couple the names of Handel and Beethoven. Handel is a kind of Beethoven in chains. He had the unapproachable manner like the great Italian artists who surrounded him : the Porporas, the Hasses, and

---

[1] Extract from a pamphlet published in London (1751) on *The art of composing music in a completely new manner adapted even to the feeblest intellects.*
Already Pope in 1742 compared Handel with Briareus.

> " Strong in new arms, lo ! Giant HANDEL stands,
>   Like bold Briareus with his *hundred hands.*"

At the time of *Rinaldo* (1711) Addison accused Handel of delighting in noise.

between him and them there was a whole world.[1]
Under the classic ideal with which he covered himself burned a romantic genius, precursor of the
Sturm und Drang period ; and sometimes this
hidden demon broke out in brusque fits of passion
—perhaps despite himself.

. . . . . .

Handel's instrumental music deserves very close
notice : for it is nearly always wrongly assessed by
historians, and badly understood by artists, who
treat it for the most part as a merely formal art.

Its chief characteristic is that of a perpetual
improvisation. If it was published, it was more in
spite of Handel than at his instigation.[2] It was not
made to be played and judged coldly, but to
be produced at white heat to the public. They were
free sketches, in which the form was never completely tightened up, but remained always moving

[1] " . . . You refuse to submit to rules ; you refuse to let your
genius be hampered by them. . . . O thou Goth and Vandal ! . . .
You also allow nightingales and canaries on the stage and let
them execute their untrained natural operas, in order that you
may be considered a composer. A carpenter with his rule and
square can go as far in composition as you, O perfect irregu-
arity ! " (*Harmony in Revolt : a letter to Frederic Handel esquire,
. . . by Hurlothrumbo-Johnson,* February, 1734).

[2] Soon Handel was obliged to publish these works, because
fraudulent and faulty copies were being sold. It was so with
the first volume of *Suites de pièces pour le clavecin,* published in
1720, and the first volume of Organ Concertos published in 1738.
Some of these publications had been made in a bare-faced manner
without Handel's permission by publishers who had pilfered
them. So it was with the second volume of *Suites de pièces pour
le clavecin,* which Walsh had appropriated and published in 1733
without giving Handel an opportunity of correcting the proofs.
It is very remarkable that, notwithstanding the great European
success achieved by the first volume for the Clavecin, Handel
did not trouble to publish the others.

and living, modifying itself at the concert, as the two sensibilities—the artist and the public—came into touch with one another.[1] It is necessary then to preserve in this music a certain measure of the character of living improvisation. What we too often do, on the contrary, is to petrify them. One cannot say that they are a caricature of the work of Handel. They are rather a negation of it. When one studies with a minute care every detail of the work, when one has attained from the orchestra a precision of attack, an ensemble, a justness, an irreproachable finish, we have yet done nothing more than raise up the mere figure of this genial improvisator.

Further, there is with his instrumental music, as with his vocal music, nearly always an intimate and picturesque expression. For Handel, as with his friend Geminiani, "the aim of instrumental music is not only to please the ear, but to express the sentiments, the emotions, to paint the feelings."[2] It reflects not only the interior world, but it also turns to the actual spectacle of things.[3] It is a

[1] All his contemporaries agree in praising the wonderful genius with which Handel adapted himself instinctively in his improvisations to the spirit of his audience. Like all the greatest Virtuosos he soon placed himself in the closest spiritual communion with his public ; and, so to speak, they collaborated together.

[2] Geminiani's Preface to his *Ecole de violon*, or *The Art of Playing on the Violin, Containing all the Rules necessary to attain to Perfection on that Instrument, with great variety of Compositions, which will also be very useful to those who study the violoncello, harpsichord, etc.* Composed by F. Geminiani, Opera IX, London, MDCCLI.

[3] Geminiani himself had attempted to represent in music the pictures of Raphael and the poems of Tasso.

precise poetry, and if one cannot define the sources of his inspiration, one can often find in certain of his instrumental works the souvenir of days and journeys, and of scenes visited and experienced by Handel. It was here that he was visibly inspired by Nature.[1]

Others have a relationship with vocal and dramatic works. Certain of the heroic fugues in the fourth book of the Clavier pieces published in 1735 were taken up again by Handel in his *Israel in Egypt* and clothed with words which agreed precisely with their hidden feeling. The first *Allegro* from the Fourth Organ Concerto (the first book appeared in 1738) soon became shortly afterwards one of the prettiest of the choruses in *Alcina*. The second and monumental concerto for two horns in F Major[2] is a reincarnation of some of the finest pages from *Esther*. It was quite evident to the public of his time that the instrumental works had an expressive meaning, or that as Geminiani wrote, " all good music ought to be an imitation of a fine discourse." Thus the publisher Walsh was justified in issuing his six volumes of Favourite Airs from Handel's operas and oratorios, arranged as *Sonatas for the flute, violin, and harpsichord*, and Handel himself, or his pupil, W. Babell, arranged excellently for the clavier, some suites of airs from the

[1] For example, the *Allegro* of the First Organ Concerto (second volume published in 1740), with its charming dialogue between the cuckoo and the nightingale, or the first of the Second Organ Concerto (in the same volume), or several of the *Concerti Grossi* (referred to later).

[2] Vol. XLVII of the Complete Handel Edition.

L

operas, binding them together with preludes, interludes, and variations.—It is necessary always to keep in view this intimate relation of the instrumental works of Handel with the rest of his music. It ought to draw our attention more and more to the expressive contents of these works.

.   .   .   .   .

The instrumental music of Handel divides itself into three classes : firstly—music for the clavier (the clavecin and organ) ; secondly—chamber music (sonatas and trios) ; thirdly—orchestral music. The compositions for clavier are the most popular works of any that Handel wrote, and these have achieved the greatest number of European editions. Although they comprise three volumes, yet there is only one, the first, which represents him properly, for it is the only one which he prepared himself, and supervised. The others, more or less fraudulently published, misrepresent him.

This First Volume, published in November, 1720, under the French title *Suites*, etc., affords us the means of appreciating the two most striking of Handel's traits : his precocious maturity, which hardly developed at all in the course of time ; and the European universality of character which distinguished his art even at an epoch when the great artists were less national than they are to-day. For the first trait one would remark in fine that these Clavier Pieces published in 1720 had already been written some time, certainly before 1700. One discovers a part of them in the *Jugendbuch* of the

Lennard Collection.[1] Others come from *Almira*, 1705. Naturally Handel enlarged and revised, and carefully grouped all these pieces in his edition of 1720. The interest of the *Jugendbuch* is chiefly that it shows us the first sketches of the pieces, and how Handel perfected them. Side by side with the oldest pieces there are others more recent, composed, it may be, in Italy or in England.[2] One can trace in these pages the course of the different influences. Seiffert and Fleischer have noted some of them,[3] German influences, French, and Italian.[4] In

---

[1] It is a manuscript of 21 pages, the writing appearing to date from about 1710. It is certainly a copy from some older works. Chrysander published it in Volume XLVIII of the Complete Edition. It is probable that Handel had given to an English friend a selection from the compositions of his early youth. They were passed from hand to hand, and were even fraudulently published, as Handel tells us himself in the Edition of 1720 : " I have been led to publish some of the following pieces, because some faulty copies of them have been surreptitiously circulated abroad." In this number appear, for example, the Third Suite, the Sarabande of the Seventh Suite, etc.

[2] It is said that Handel wrote these for the Princess Anne, whom he taught the clavecin ; but Chrysander had observed that the princess was only eleven years old at the time. It is more probable that these pieces were written for the Duke of Chandos or for the Duke of Burlington.—It is in the second book of Clavier Pieces that we find the much easier pieces written for the princesses.

[3] In their republication of the *Geschichte der Klaviermusik* by Weitzmann (1899), in which the chapter devoted to Handel contains the fullest information of any description of the Clavier works.

[4] Influences of Krieger and of Kuhnau, particularly in the Halle period (see Vol. XLVIII, pp. 146, 149) ; French influences in the Hamburg Period (pp. 166, 170) ; influences of Pasquini (p. 162) ; and of Scarlatti (pp. 148, 152), about the time of his Italian visits. The influence of Kuhnau is very marked, and Handel had all his life a well-stocked memory of this music, and particularly of Kuhnau's *Klavier-Uebung* (1689–1692), and the *Frischen Klavier-Früchte* (1696), which were then widely known and published in numerous editions. Here is the same limpid

England even, sometimes Italian elements, sometimes German, predominated with him.[1] The order of the dances varies in each Suite, and also the central point, the kernel of the work. The introductory pieces are sometimes preludes, sometimes fugues, overtures, etc. The dances and the airs are sometimes related to one another, and sometimes independent, and nevertheless the prevailing impression of the work, so varied in its texture, is its complete unity. The personality of Handel holds it all together and welds the most diverse elements —polyphony and richness of German harmony, Italian homophony, and Scarlattian technique, the French rhythm and ornamentation[2] with English directness and practicability. Thus the work made its impression on the times. Before this time, there had perhaps been more original volumes of pieces for the clavier, but their inspiration was nearly always very much circumscribed by the limits of their national art. Handel was the first of the great German classics of the eighteenth century. He did for music what the French writers and philosophers of the eighteenth century did for literature. He wrote for all and sundry, and his volume took the

style, the same neat soberness of line. Kuhnau's Sarabandes especially are already completely Handelian. It is the same with certain Preludes, certain Gigues, and some of the airs (a trifle popular). *

[1] For the German influence, see the Suites 1, 4, 5, 8 (four dance movements preceded by an introduction). For the Italian, see the Suites 2, 3, 6, 7, of which the form approximates to the *Sonata da camera.*

[2] M. Seiffert adds that none of these elements predominate. I would rather follow the opinion of Chrysander, who notices in this fusion of three national styles a predominant tendency to the Italian, just as Bach inclines most to the French style.

place on the day of its publication which it has held since, that of a European classic.

The following volumes are less interesting for the reasons I have given. The Second Volume published in 1733 by Walsh, *unknown* to Handel, and in a very faulty manner, gives us little pieces which we find in the *Jugendbuch*, and which date from the time of Hamburg and Halle.[1] They lack the setting which Handel had certainly planned for them : preludes and fugues.

This arrangement was ready ; and Handel, frustrated by this publisher, resigned himself to publishing them later on, as an Appendix to the preceding work : *Six Fugues or Voluntaries for the Organ or Harpsichord*, 1735, *Opus* 3. These fugues date from the time when Handel was at Canons before 1720, the second in G Major was from the period of his first sojourn in England. They became celebrated at once, and were much circulated in

---

[1] One finds there, cycles of variations on Minuets, on Gavottes, especially on Chaconnes and many other Italian forms. The Gigue of the Sixth Suite (in G minor) comes from an air in *Almira* (1705). One notices also that the Eighth Suite in G major is in the French style (particularly the Gavotte in rondo with five variations).

It is necessary to follow this second volume by the third, which contains works of widely different periods : *Fantasia, Capriccio, Preludio e Allegro, Sonata*, published at Amsterdam in 1732, and dating from his youthful period (the Second Suite was inspired by an *Allemande* of Mattheson) : *Lessons composed for the Princess Louisa* (when aged twelve or thirteen years) about 1736 ; *Capriccio in G minor* (about the same date) ; and *Sonata in C major* in 1750.

Finally, there should be added to these volumes, various clavier works published in Vol. XLVIII of the Complete Edition under the title : *Klaviermusik und Cembalo Bearbeitungen*. There is also a selection of the best arrangements of symphonies and airs from the operas of Handel by Babell (about 1713 or 1714).

manuscript even in Germany.[1] Handel had trained
himself in fugue in the school of Kuhñau, and
specially with Johann Krieger.[2] Like them he
gave his Fugues an essentially melodic character.
They are so suited for singing that two of them,
as we have said, afterwards served for two
choruses in the first part of *Israel*,[3] but Handel's
compositions possess a far different vitality from
that of his German forerunners. They have a
charming intrepidity, a fury, a passion, a fire which
belongs only to him. In other words they live. "All
the notes talk," says Mattheson. These fugues
have the character of happy improvisations, and in
truth they were improvised. Handel calls them
Voluntaries, that is fanciful and learned caprices.
He made frequent use of double fugues with a
masterly development. "Such an art rejoices the
hearer and warms the heart towards the composer
and towards the executant," says Mattheson again,
who, after having heard J. S. Bach, found Handel
the greater in the composition of the double fugue
and in improvisation. This habit of Handel—one
might say almost a craving—for improvising, was the
origin of the grand Organ Concertos. After the
fashion of his time, Handel conducted his operas
and oratorios from the clavier. He accompanied

---

[1] Mattheson in 1722 quoted the Fugue in E minor as quite a
recent work.

[2] Handel himself told his friend Bernard Granville so, when
he made him a present of Krieger's work : *Anmuthige Clavier-
Uebung*, published in 1699.

[3] The Fugue in A minor was used for the Chorus, *He smote all
the firstborn in Egypt*, in *Israel in Egypt*, and the Fugue in G
minor. The Chorus, *They loathed to drink at the river*. Another
(the 4th) served for the Overture to the *Passion after Brockes*.

the singers with a marvellous art, blending himself to their fancy, and when the singer had done, he delivered his version.[1] From the interludes on the clavier in his operas, he passed to the fantasies or caprices on the organ in the *entr'actes* of his oratorios, and his success was so great that he never again abandoned this custom. One might say that the public were drawn to his oratorios more by his improvisations on the organ than by the oratorios themselves. Two volumes of the Organ Concertos were published during the lifetime of Handel, in 1738 and in 1740 ; the third a little after his death, in 1760.[2]

To judge them properly it is necessary to bear in

[1] The indications: *ad libitum*, or *cembalo*, found time after time in his scores, marked the places reserved for the improvisation.

Despite Handel's great physical power, his touch was extraordinarily smooth and equal. Burney tells us that when he played, his fingers were " so curved and compact, that no motion, and scarcely the fingers themselves, could be discovered " (*Commemoration of Handel*, p. 35). M. Seiffert believes that " his technique, which realised all Rameau's principles, certainly necessitated the use of the thumb in the modern style," and that " one can trace a relationship between Handel's arrival in England and the adoption of the Italian fingering which soon became fully established there."

[2] A fourth was published by Arnold in 1797 ; but part of the works which it contains are not original. Handel had nothing to do with the publication of the Second Set.

Vol. XXVIII of the Complete Edition contains the Six Concertos of the First Set, Op. 4 (1738) and the Six of the Third Set, Op. 7 (1760). Vol. XLVIII comprises the concertos of the Second Set (1740), an experiment at a Concerto for two organs and orchestra, and two Concertos from the Fourth Set (1797).

Many of the Concertos are dated. Most of them were written between 1735 and 1751 ; and several for special occasions ; the sixth of the First Set for an *entr'acte* to *Alexander's Feast ;* the fourth of the First Set, a little before *Alcina ;* the third of the Third Set for the Foundling Hospital. The Concerto in B minor (No. 3) was always associated in the mind of the English public with *Esther ;* for the minuet was called the " Minuet from Esther."

mind that they were destined for the theatre. It would be absurd to expect works in the strict, vigorous, and involved style of J. S. Bach. They were brilliant *divertissements*, of which the style, somewhat commonplace yet luminous and pompous, preserves the character of oratorio improvisations, finding their immediate effect on the great audience. " *When he gave a concerto,*" says Hawkins, " *his method in general was to introduce it with a voluntary movement on the diapasons, which stole on the ear in a slow and solemn progression ; the harmony close wrought, and as full as could possibly be expressed ; the passages concatenated with stupendous art, the whole at the same time being perfectly intelligible, and carrying the appearance of great simplicity. This kind of prelude was succeeded by the concerto itself, which he executed with a degree of spirit and firmness that no one can ever pretend to equal.*" Even at the height of the cabal which was organised against Handel, the Grub Street Journal published an enthusiastic poem on Handel's Organ Concertos.[1]

> " *Oh winds, softly, softly raise your golden wings*
>   *among the branches !*
> *That all may be silent, make even the whisperings of*
>   *Zephyrs to cease.*
> *Sources of life, suspend your course. . . .*
> *Listen, listen, Handel the incomparable plays ! . . .*
> *Oh look, when he, the powerful man, makes the forces*
>   *of the organ resound,*
> *Joy assembles its cohorts, malice is appeased, . . .*
> *His hand, like that of the Creator, conducts his noble*
>   *work with order, with grandeur and reason. . . .*
> *Silence, bunglers in art ! It is nothing here to have*
>   *the favour of great lords. Here, Handel is king.*"

[1] May 8, 1735. It was the year when Handel wrote and performed his first Concertos of the First Set.

It is necessary then to view these Organ Concertos in the proper sense of magnificent concerts for a huge public.[1] Great shadows, great lights, strong and joyous contrasts, all are conceived in view of a colossal effect. The orchestra usually consists of two oboes, two violins, viola, and basses (violoncellos, bassoons, and cembalo), occasionally two flutes, some contrabassos and a harp.[2] The concertos are in three or four movements, which are generally connected in pairs. Usually they open with a *pomposo*, or a *staccato*, in the style of the French overture,[3] often an *allegro* in the same style follows. For the conclusion, an *allegro moderato*, or an *andante*, somewhat animated, sometimes some dances. The *adagio* in the middle is often missing, and is left to be improvised on the organ. The form has a certain relation with that of the sonata in three movements, *allegro-adagio-allegro*, preceded by an introduction. The first pieces of these two first concertos published in Volume XLVIII of the

[1] Hawkins wrote further : " Music was less fashionable than it is now, many of both sexes were ingenuous enough to confess that they wanted this sense, by saying, ' I have no ear for music.' Persons such as these, who, had they been left to themselves, would have interrupted the hearing of others by their talking, were by the performance of Handel not only charmed into silence, but were generally the loudest in their acclamations. This, though it could not be said to be genuine applause, was a much stronger proof of the power of harmony, than the like effect on an audience composed only of judges and rational admirers of his art " (*General History of Music*, p. 912).

[2] In the Tenth Concerto there are two violoncellos and two bassoons. The same in the Concerto for two Organs. In the long Concerto in F major (Vol. XLVIII) we find two horns.

[3] Sometimes the name is found marked there. See the Eighth Concerto in Vol. XXVIII and the Concerto in F major in Vol. XLVIII.

Complete Edition (second volume) are in a picturesque and descriptive style. The long Concerto
in F Major in the same volume has the swing of
festival music, very closely allied to the open-air
style. Finally, one must notice the beautiful
experiment, unfortunately not continued, of the
Concerto for two organs,[1] and that, more astonishing still, of a Concerto for Organ terminated by
a Chorus,[2] thus opening the way for Beethoven's
fine Symphony, and to his successors, Berlioz, Liszt,
and Mahler.[3]

.   .   .   .   .   .

The chamber music of Handel proves to be of the
same precocious maturity as his clavier music.

Six Sonatas in Trio for two oboes and harpsichord[4]
appear to date from about 1696, when he was eleven
years old, and while he was still at Halle, where he
wrote as he said, " like the devil," above all for the
oboe, his favourite instrument. They are in four
movements : *adagio, allegro, adagio, allegro.* The
slow movements are often very short, and the
second between them is sometimes a mere transition. The Sonata for *Viola da Gamba*, and

---

[1] Vol. XLVIII, page 51.

[2] Mr. Streatfeild was, I believe, the first to notice an autograph MS. of the Fourth Organ Concerto to which is attached
a Hallelujah Chorus built on a theme from the concerto itself.
This MS., which is found at the British Museum, dates from
1735, and appears to have been used for the revival in 1737 of
the *Trionfo del Tempo* to which the Concerto serves for conclusion.

[3] Scriabin also.—*Translator.*

[4] *Six Sonatas or Trios for two Hoboys with a thorough bass for
the Harpsichord.* Published in Vol. XXVII.

Cembalo Concertato in C Major[1] probably belongs to 1705, when Handel was at Hamburg. It is the only one of its kind in the works of Handel, which shows him as a forerunner of Bach. The sonata is in trio form. The clavier plays a second *obbligato* besides the bass part, as Seiffert notes: " Ten years before Bach worked at his Sonatas with accompaniment for *cembalo obbligato,* Handel had already a clear perception of their value."

Three Sonatas for Flute and Bass,[2] of an elegiac grace, also perhaps date from the Halle period, and according to Chrysander seem to have been continued up to 1710 at Hanover.

But the chief instrumental chamber works written by Handel were published in London between 1732 and 1740, and they comprise three volumes :[3]

(1) Fifteen sonatas or solos for a German flute, oboe or violin, with a thorough bass for the harpsichord, or bass violin, Op. 1.

(2) Nine sonatas or trios for two violins, flutes, or oboes, with a thorough bass for the harpsichord, or violoncello, Op. 2.

(3) Seven sonatas or trios for two violins, or German flutes, with a thorough bass for the harpsichord, or violoncello, Op. 5.

The first volume contains very old pieces, of which some date from the time when Handel was at

---

[1] Volume XLVIII, page 112.
[2] Volume XLVIII, page 130.
[3] Volume XXVII.

Burlington and Chandos. Others might have been intended for the Prince of Wales, whose violin teacher, John Dubourg, was a friend of Handel, as they date from about 1730. The second volume appeared at first in Amsterdam, afterwards in London with Walsh, under a French title[1] in 1733.

The third volume was composed in 1738, and published about the beginning of 1739.[2]

The first feature to notice in general is the want of definition in the choice of instruments for which this music was written. Following the same abstract æsthetic of his time, the composer left it to the players to choose the instruments. However, there was no doubt that in the first conception of Handel certain of these pieces were made for the flute, others for the violin, and others for the oboe.

In the volume Op. 1 of the solo sonatas (for the flute or oboe, or violin) with bass (harpsichord or violoncello), the usual form is generally in four movements:[3] *adagio, allegro, adagio, allegro.* The slow pieces are very short. Several are inspired by the airs of Italian cantatas and operas. Some of the pieces are joined together.[4] The harmony is often thin, and requires to be filled in.

---

[1] *VII Sonatas à 2 violons, 2 hautbois, ou 2 flûtes traversières et basse continue, composées par G. F. Handel, Second ouvrage.*

[2] Later on, Walsh made arrangements of favourite airs from Handel's Operas and Oratorios as " Sonatas " for flute, violin and harpsichord. Six Vols.

[3] In eleven sonatas out of sixteen. One sonata (the third) is in three movements. Three are in five movements (the first, the fifth and the seventh). One is in seven movements (the ninth).

[4] In the first Sonata, the final *Presto* in common time uses the theme of the *Andante* in 3–4, which forms the second movement. In the second Sonata, the final *Presto* in common time is built on the subject of the *Andante* in 3–4, slightly modified.

The second and third volumes have a much
greater value, containing trios or sonatas in two
parts (for two violins, or two oboes, or two *flauti-
traversi*) with Bass (harpsichord or violoncello). All
the sonatas in the second volume, with only one
exception,[1] have four movements, two slow and
two fast alternatively, as in the Opus 1. Sometimes
they are inspired by the airs of the operas, or of the
oratorios; at other times they have furnished a
brief sketch for them. The elegiac *Largo* which
opens the First Sonata is found again in *Alessandro*,
the *allegro* which finishes the Third Sonata forms
one of the movements in the overture of *Athaliah*,
the larghetto of the Fourth serves for the second
movement of the *Esther* overture. Other pieces
have been transferred to the clavier or other
instrumental works, where they are joined to other
movements. The finest of these Trios are the First
and the Ninth, both of enchanting poetry. In the
second movement of the Ninth Trio, Handel has
utilised very happily a popular English theme.

The Seven Trios from the third volume afford a
much greater variety in the style and in the number[2]
of the pieces. Dances occupy a great part.[3] They
are indeed veritable Suites. They were composed
in the years when Handel was attracted by the

---

[1] The fifth Sonata is in five movements—*larghetto, allegro*
(3–8), *adagio, allegro* (4–4), *allegro* (12–8).

[2] From five to seven movements.

[3] A Gavotte concludes the first, second, and third trios. A
Minuet ends the fourth, sixth, and seventh. A Bourrée finishes
the fifth. There are also found two Musettes and a March in
the second Trio, a Sarabande, an Allemande and a Rondo in
the third; a Passacaille and a Gigue in the fourth.

form of ballet-opera. The Musette and the *Allegro*
of the Second Sonata come from *Ariodante*. Some
of the other slow and pompous movements are
borrowed from his oratorios. The two *Allegri* which
open the Fourth Sonata are taken from the Overture of *Athaliah*. On the other hand, Handel inserts
in the final movement of *Belshazzar* the beautiful
Andante which opens his First Sonata.

Whoever wishes to judge these works historically
or from the intellectual point of view, will find, like
Chrysander, that Handel has not invented here any
new forms, and, as he advanced, he returned to the
form of the Suite, which already belonged to the
past, instead of continuing on his way towards the
future Sonata. But those who will judge them
artistically, for their own personal charm, will find
in them some of the purest creations of Handel, and
those which best retain their freshness. Their
beautiful Italian lines, their delicate expression,
their aristocratic simplicity, are refreshing alike to
the mind and to the heart. Our own epoch, tired of
the post-Beethoven and post-Wagnerian art, can
find here, as in the chamber music of Mozart, a
safe haven, where it can escape the sterile agitation
of the present and find again quiet peace and
sanity.

.   .   .   .   .

The orchestral music of Handel comprises twelve
Concerti Grossi (1740), the six Oboe Concertos (1734),
the Symphonies from his operas, oratorios, and
his open-air music—Water-Music (1715 or 1717),

Firework Music (1749),—and *Concerti* for two horns.

Although Handel was in art a visualist, and though his music had a highly descriptive and evocatory power, he only made a very restrained use of instrumental tone-colour.[1] However, he showed on occasion a refined intelligence in its use. The two oratorios written at Rome when he found himself in the society of the Cardinal Ottoboni, and his great *virtuoso* works, *The Triumph of Time* and *The Resurrection* of 1708, have a fine and well-varied orchestration.[2] In London he was one of the first to introduce the use of the horn into the orchestra of the opera.[3] " He was the first," says Volbach, " to assert the expressive personality of

---

[1] It was the æsthetic of the period. Thus M. Mennicke writes : " Neutrality of orchestral colour characterises the time of Bach and Handel. The instrumentation corresponds to the registration of an Organ." The Symphonic orchestra is essentially built up on the strings. The wind instruments serve principally as *ripieno*. When they used the wood-wind *obbligato*, it went on throughout the movement and did not merely add a touch of colour here and there.

[2] One finds in the middle of the *Trionfo del Tempo* an instrumental Sonata for 2 Oboes, 2 Violins, Viola, Cello, Basso, and Organ. In the Solo of the Magdalene in the *Resurrection*, Handel uses two flutes, two violins (muted), *viola da gamba* and cello ; the cello is occupied with a pedal-note of thirty-nine bars at the opening, and then joins the clavecin. In the middle of the air, the *viola da gamba* and the flutes play by themselves.

[3] In *Radamisto* (1720) Tiridate's air : *Alzo al colo*, and final chorus. In *Giulio Cesare*, 4 horns.

I do not suppose that Handel was the first to use the clarinets in an orchestra, as this appears very doubtful. One sees on a copy of *Tamerlano* by Schmidt : *clar. e clarini* (in place of the *cornetti* in the autograph manuscript). But it is feasible that just as with the " *clarinettes* " used by Rameau in the *Acanthe et Céphise*, the high trumpets are intended. Mr. Streatfeild mentions also a concerto for two " clarinets " and *corno di caccia*, the MS. being in the Fitzwilliam Museum at Cambridge.

the violoncello.''[1]   From the viola he knew how to
secure many curious effects of indefinite and
disquieting half-tones,[2] he gave to the bassoons a
lugubrious and fantastic character,[3] he experimented with new instruments, small[4] and great,[5]
he used the drum (*tambour*) solo in a dramatic
fashion for Jupiter's oath in *Semele*. For special
situations, by instrumental tone-colours, he secures
effects not only of dramatic expression, but also of
exotism and local colour.   It is so in the two scenes
from the two Cleopatras, *Giulio Cesare* (1724) and
Alexander Balus (1748).

[1] *Alcina, Semele, L'Allegro, Alexander's Feast*, the little *Ode
to St. Cecilia*, etc.   Usually Handel imparts to the cello either
an amorous desire or an elegiac consolation.

[2] Thus, in the famous scene which opens the second Act of *Alexander's Feast* (second part of the air in G minor), evoking the host
of the dead who have wandered at night from their graves, there
are no violins, no brass ; just 3 bassoons, 2 violas, cello, bassi
and organ.

[3] In *Saul*, the scene of the Sorcerer, apparition of the spirit
of Samuel.

[4] The *violette marine* (little violas very soft) in *Orlando* (1733).

[5] The monster instruments used for the colossal performances
at Westminster.   The double bassoon by Stainsby made in 1727
for the coronation celebrations.   Handel borrowed from the
Captain of Artillery some huge drums preserved at the Tower
of London, for *Saul* and for the *Dettingen Te Deum*.   Moreover,
like Berlioz, he was not afraid of using firearms in the orchestra.
Mrs. Elizabeth Carter wrote : " Handel has literally introduced
firearms into *Judas Maccabæus* ; and they have a good effect "
(*Carter Correspondence*, p. 134), and Sheridan, in a humorous
sketch (Jupiter) represents an author who directs a pistol-shot
to be fired behind the scenes, as saying, " See, I borrowed this
from Handel."

[6] For the scene of Cleopatra's apparition on the Parnassus,
at the opening of Act II of *Giulio Cesare*, Handel has two orchestras, one on the stage ; Oboe, 2 Violins, Viola, Harp, Viola
da gamba, Theorbo, Bassoons, Cellos ; the other, in front.   The
first air of Cleopatra in *Alexander Balus* is accompanied by 2
Flutes, 2 Violins, Viola,' 2 Cellos, Harp, Mandoline, Basses, Bassoon
and Organ.

But great painter as Handel was he did not work
so much through the brilliancy, variety, and
novelty of his tone-colours as by the beauty of his
designs, and his effects of light and shade. With a
voluntarily restrained palette, and by satisfying
himself with the sober colours of the strings, he yet
was able to produce surprising and thrilling effects.
Volbach has shown[1] that he had less recourse to the
contrast and mixing of instruments than to the
division of the same family of instruments into
different groups. In the introductory piece movement to his second *Esther* (1732) the violins are
divided into five groups ;[2] in *The Resurrection*
(1708), into four divisions ;[3] the violas are sometimes divided into two, the second being reinforced
by the third violin, or by the violoncellos.[4] On
the other hand, Handel, when he considered it
advisable, reduced his instrumental forces by
suppressing the viola and the second violin, whose
places were taken by the clavecin. All his
orchestral art is in the true instinct of balance and
economy, which, with the most restricted means in
managing a few colours, yet knows how to obtain as
powerful impressions as our musicians of to-day,
with their crowded palette.[5] Nothing, then, is more

[1] Fritz Volbach : *Die Praxis der Handel-Auffahrung*, 1899.

[2] In addition to two parts for Flutes, two for Oboes, two for
Bassoons, Violas, Cellos and Basses, Cembalo, Theorbo, Harp and
Organ ; in all, fifteen orchestral parts to accompany a single
voice of *Esther*.

[3] For the Angel's Song.

[4] In *Saul*, " *viola II per duoi violoncelli ripieni.*" (See Volbach,
ibid.)

[5] Study from this point of view the progress from the very
simple instrumentation of *Alexander's Feast*, where at first two

M

important, if we wish to render this music truly, than the avoidance of upsetting the equilibrium of the various sections of the orchestra under the pretext of enriching it and bringing it up to date. The worse fault is to deprive it, by a useless surplus of tone-colours, of that suppleness and subtlety of nuance which is its principal charm.

One is prone to accept too readily the idea, that expressive nuance is a privilege of the modern musical art, and that Handel's orchestra knew only the great theatrical contrasts between force and sweetness, or loudness and softness. It is nothing of the kind. The range of Handel's nuances is extremely varied. One finds with him the *pianissimo*, the *piano*, the *mezzo piano*, the *mezzo forte*, *un poco più F*, *un poco F*, *forte*, *fortissimo*. We never find the orchestral *crescendo* and *decrescendo*, which hardly appears marked expressly until the time of Jommelli,[1] and the school of Mannheim; but there is no doubt that it was practised long before it was marked in the music.[2] The President of Brosses wrote in 1739 from Rome : " The voices, like the violins, used with light and shade, with unconscious swelling of sound, which augments the force from note to note, even to a very high degree,

Oboes are used with the strings, then appear successively two Bassoons (air No. 6), two Horns (air No. 9), two Trumpets and Drums (Part II), and, for conclusion, with the heavenly apparition of St. Cecilia, two Flutes.

[1] Dr. Hermann Abert has found the first indication : *crescendo il forte* in Jommelli's *Artaserse*, performed at Rome in 1749. In the eighteenth century the Abbé Vogler and Schubart already had attributed the invention of the *Crescendo* to Jommelli.

[2] See Lucien Kamiensky : *Mannheim und Italien* (*Sammelbände der I.M.G.*, January–March, 1909).

since its use as a nuance is extremely sweet and
touching." And endless examples occur in Handel
of long *crescendi* and *diminuendi* without its
expression being marked in the scores.[1] Another
kind of *crescendo* and *diminuendo* on the same note
was very common in the time of Handel, and his
friend, Geminiani, helped to set the fashion.
Volbach, and with him Hugo Riemann,[2] has shown
that Geminiani used in the later editions of his first
Violin Sonatas in 1739, and in his Violin School in
1751, the two following signs :

Swelling the sound [ˈ]

Diminishing (falling) the sound [ˈ]

As Geminiani explains it, " The sound ought to
commence softly, and should swell out in a gradual
fashion to about half its value, then it should
diminish to the end. The movement of the bow
should continue without interruption."

It happens thus, that by a refinement of expression, which became a mannerism of the Mannheim
school, but which also became a source of powerful

---

[1] M. Volbach has noticed in the overture to the *Choice of
Hercules*, second movement: *piano, mezzo forte, un poco più
forte, forte, mezzo piano*, all in fourteen bars. In the chorus in
Acis and Galatea, " Mourn, all ye muses," one reads *forte, piano,
pp.*—The introduction of *Zadock the Priest* shows a colossal
crescendo ; the introductory movement to the final chorus in
Deborah, a very broad *diminuendo*.

[2] H. Riemann : *Zur Herkunft der dynamischen Schwellzeichen*
(I.M.G., February, 1909).

contrast with the Beethovenians, the swelling
stopped short of its aim, and was followed instead
by a sudden piano, as in the following example from
the Trio Sonatas of Geminiani.

It is more than probable that the virtuoso
players of Handel's orchestra also used this means
of expression,[1] though we need not assume that
Handel used them as abundantly as Geminiani or
as the Mannheim players, whose taste had become
doubtless a little affected and exaggerated. But
what is certain is that with him, as with Geminiani,
and indeed with all the great artists of his time,
especially with the Italians and their followers,
music was a real discourse, and ought to be rendered
with inflections as free and as varied as natural
speech.[2]

How was it possible to realise all the suppleness
and subtleties of elocution on the orchestra ?   To

[1] Carle Mennicke notices the same sign for *decrescendo* (($>$))
on a long note in the Overture to Rameau's *Acanthe et Céphise*
(1751).

[2] Geminiani says of the *forte* and the *piano :* " They are
absolutely necessary to give expression to the melody ; for all
good music being the imitation of a fine discourse, these two
ornaments have for their aim the varied inflections of the
speaking voice." Telemann writes : " Song is the foundation of
music, in every way. What the instruments play ought to be
exactly after the principles of expression in singing."

And M. Volbach shows that these principles governed music
then in Germany with all kinds of musicians, even with the
trompettist Altenburg, whose *School for the Trumpet* was based
on the principle that instrumental performance ought to be
similar to vocal rendering.

HANDEL DIRECTING AN ORATORIO.

Handel is seen (on the left) seated at a cembalo with two keyboards in the midst of his musicians. At his right hand he has the "concertino" group (consisting of the 'cellist, two violinists and two flautists). On his near left (quite close to the cembalo) are the vocal soloists. The rest of the instrumentalists are out of his sight.

To face page 165.]

understand this it is necessary to examine the disposition and placing of the orchestra of that time. It was not, as with us, centralised under the control of a single conductor. Thus, as Seiffert tells us,[1] in Handel's time it was the principle of decentralisation which ruled. The choruses had their leaders, who listened to the organ, from which they took their cue, and so sustained the voices. The orchestra was divided into three sections, after the Italian method. Firstly, the *Concertino*, comprising a first and a second violin, and a solo violoncello ; secondly, the *Concerto Grosso*, comprising the instrumental choir ; thirdly, the *Ripienists* strengthening the *Grosso*.[2]

A picture in the British Museum, representing Handel in the midst of his musicians, depicts the composer seated at the clavier (a cembalo with two keyboards, of which the lid is raised). He is surrounded by the violoncellist (placed at his right-hand side), two violins and two flutes, which are placed just before him, under his eye. The solo singers are also near him, on his left, quite close to the clavecin. The rest of the instrumentalists are

---

[1] Max Seiffert : *Die Verzierung der Sologesange in Haendels Messias (Sammelbände der I.M.G.*, July–September, 1907).

[2] Fritz Volbach reckons for the *Concerto Grosso*, 8 first violins, 8 seconds, 6 violas, 4 to 6 cellos, 4 basses—and for the *Ripienists*, 6 first violins, 6 seconds, 4 violas, 3 or 4 celli, and 3 basses.

These numbers are much greater than that of Handel's own performances. The programmes of a performance of the *Messiah* at the Foundling Hospital, May 3, 1759, a little after Handel's death, give only 56 executants, of which 33 were instrumentalists and 23 singers. The orchestra was divided into 12 violins, 3 violas, 3 cellos, 4 oboes, 4 bassoons, 2 trumpets, 2 horns and drums (see *Musical Times*, May, 1902).

behind him, out of his sight. Thus his directions and
his glances would control the *Concertino,* who would
transmit in their turn the chief conductor's wishes
to the *Concerto Grosso,* and they in their turn to the
Ripienists. In place of the quasi-military discipline
of modern orchestras, controlled under the baton
of a chief conductor, the different bodies of the
Handelian orchestra governed one another with
elasticity, and it was the incisive rhythm of the
little *Cembalo* which put the whole mass into
motion. Such a method avoided the mechanical
stiffness of our performances. The danger was
rather a certain wobbling without the powerful and
infectious will-power of a chief such as Handel, and
without the close sympathy of thought which was
established between him and his capable sub-
conductors of the *Concertino* and of the *Grosso.*

It is this elasticity which should be aimed at in
the instrumental works of Handel when they are
executed nowadays.[1]

.   .   .   .   .   .

We will first take his *Concerti Grossi.*[2] None of
his works are more celebrated and less understood.

---

[1] " *Leichtigkeit der Bewegung und Beweglichkeit des Aus-
drucks,*" as Volbach tells us (suppleness of time and fluidity of
expression) ; these are the essential qualities which alone will
revive the true rendering of Handel's works.

[2] 12 *Grand Concertos* for stringed instruments and clavier
(Vol. XXX of the Complete Edition), written from September
29 to October 20, 1739, between the little *Ode to St. Cecilia* and
L'Allegro. They appeared in April, 1740. Another volume, of
which we will speak later, is known under the name of *Oboe
Concertos,* and contains six *Concerti Grossi* (Vol. XXI of the
Complete Edition). Max Seiffert has published a well-edited
practical edition of these concertos (Breitkopf).

Handel attached to them a particular value, for he published them himself by subscription, a means which was usual in his day, but which he himself never adopted except under exceptional circumstances.

One knows that the kind of *Concerti Grossi*, which consists chiefly in a dialogue between a group of solo instrumentalists (the *Concertino*) and the full body of instruments (*Concerto Grosso*), to which is added the cembalo,[1] was, if not invented, at least carried to its perfection and rendered classical by Corelli.[2] The works of Corelli, aided by the efforts of his followers, had become widely known in Europe. Geminiani introduced them into England,[3] and without doubt Handel did not hesitate to profit by the example of Geminiani, who was his friend;[4] but it is much more natural to think that he learnt the *Concerto Grosso*, at its source at Rome, from Corelli himself during his sojourn there in 1708. Several of his Concertos in his Opus 3[5] date from

[1] The *Concertino* consists of a trio for two violins and bass *soli*, with *Cembalo Obbligato*. The Germans introduced wood-wind into the *concertino*, combining thus a violin, an oboe, a bassoon. The Italians remained faithful, generally speaking, to the stringed instruments alone.

[2] The *Concerti Grossi*, Op. 6, of Corelli, published in 1712, represent his lifelong practice. About 1682, George Moffat, visiting Rome, sought to make acquaintance there with the *Concerti Grossi* of Corelli, who already wrote them for instrumental masses of considerable size. Burney speaks of a concert of 150 string instruments conducted by Corelli at the Palace of Christine of Sweden in 1680 (see Arnold Schering's excellent little book : *Geschichte des Instrumentalkonzerts*, 1905, Breitkopf).

[3] Geminiani caused three volumes of Corelli's Concertos to be published : Op. 2 (1732), Op. 3 (1735), Op. 7 (1748).

[4] Arnold Schering has noted the relationship between a subject of Geminiani and one in Handel's *Concerto Grosso*, No. 4.

[5] Volume XXI of the Complete Edition.

1710, 1716, 1722. The same feature shows itself right up to the time of his apprenticeship at Hamburg : in any case he might have already known the Corellian style, thanks to the propaganda of George Moffat, who spread this style very early in Germany.[1] After Corelli, Locatelli,[2] and especially Vivaldi,[3] have singularly transformed the *Concerto Grosso* by giving it the free character of programme music[4] and by turning it resolutely towards the form of the Sonata in three parts. But when the works of Vivaldi were played in London in 1723, and the works which aroused such a general enthusiasm became thoroughly known to Handel, it was always to Corelli that he gave the preference, and he was very conservative in certain ways even about him. The form of his Concerto, of which the principal movements varied from four to six, oscillated between the Suite and the Sonata, and even glanced

[1] About 1682, Moffat published at Salzburg his *Armonico tributo*, Chamber Sonatas, where he mingled the style of the Lullian Trio with the style of the Italian *Concertino*. And in 1701, at Passau, he published some *Concerti Grossi* in the Italian manner after the example of Corelli.

[2] *Concerti Grossi*, Amsterdam, 1721.

[3] Antonio Vivaldi of Venice (1680–1743), choirmaster of the Ospedale della Pieta from 1714, began to be known in Germany between 1710 and 1720. The arrangements of his *Concerti Grossi*, which J. S. Bach made, date from the time when Bach was at Weimar, that is between 1708 and 1714.

[4] Locatalli and Vivaldi came under the influence of the Italian Opera. Vivaldi himself wrote thirty-eight operas. One of the *Concerti* of Locatalli (Op. 7, 1741) was named *Il pianto d' Arianna*. In the *Cimento dell' Armonia* of Vivaldi four Concertos describe the four seasons, a fifth paints *La Tempesta*, a sixth *Il Piacere* (Pleasure). In Vivaldi's Op. 10 a Concerto represents *La Notte* (Night), another *Il Cardellino* (The Goldfinch). And Arnold Schering notices Vivaldi's influence in Germany on a Graupuer at Darmstadt, and on Jos. Gregorius Werner in Bohemia.

towards the symphonic overture. It is this for
which the theorists blame him, and it is this for
which I praise him. For he does not seek to impose
a uniform cast on his thoughts, but leaves it open
to himself to fashion the form as he requires, and
the framework varies accordingly, following his
inclinations from day to day. The spontaneity of
his thought, which has already been shown by the
extreme rapidity with which the *Concerti* were
composed—each in a single day at a single sitting,
and many each week[1]—constitutes the great charm
of these works. They are, in the words of Kretzschmar, grand impression pictures, translated into
a form, at the same time precise and supple, in
which the least change of emotion can make itself
easily felt. Truly they are not all of equal value.
Their conception itself, which depended in a way on
mere momentary inspiration, is the explanation of
this extreme inequality. One ought to acknowledge
here that the Seventh Concerto, for example (the one
in B flat major), and the last three have but a
moderate interest.[2] They are amongst those least

[1] See the following dates : September 29, 1739, Concerto I in
G major ; October 4, Concerto II in F major ; October 6,
Concerto III in E minor ; October 8, Concerto IV in A minor ;
October 12, Concerto VII in B flat major ; October 15, Concerto
VI in G minor ; October 18, Concerto VIII in C minor ; October
20, Concerto XII in B minor ; October 22, Concerto X in D
minor ; October 30, Concerto XI in A major (Vol. XXX of
Complete Edition).

[2] One sees French influences particularly in the Tenth Concerto (in D minor), which has an Overture (*Grave* in 4–4 time and
Fugue in 6–8). The whole movement preserves an abstract and
irregular character. The last of the six movements—an *Allegro
Moderato*, with Variations (very pretty)—resembles a tune for a
musical box.

played; but to be quite just we must pay homage
to these masterpieces, and especially to the Second
Concerto in F major, which is like a Beethovenian
concerto : for we find there some of the spirit of
the Bonn master. For Kretzschmar the ensemble
calls to mind a beautiful autumn day—the morning,
where the rising sun pierces its way through the
clouds—the afternoon, the joyful walk, the rest in
the forest, and finally the happy and belated return.
It is difficult in fact not to have natural scenes
brought before one's eyes in hearing these works.
The first *Andante Larghetto*, which predicts, at times,
the Pastoral Symphony of Beethoven, is a reverie
on a beautiful summer's day. The spirit lulls itself
with nature's murmur, becomes intoxicated with it,
and goes to rest. The tonality rocks between
F major to B flat major and G minor. To render
this piece well it is necessary to give the time
plenty of play, often retarding it, and following
the composer's reverie in a spirit of soft leisurely
abandon.

The *Allegro* in D minor which follows is a spirited and delicate little play, a dialogue leaping from the two solo violins of the *Concerto*, then on to the *Concertino* and the *Grosso* in turn. There, also, certain passages in the Bass, robust, rollicking, and rustic, again bring to mind the Pastoral Symphony.

The third movement, a *Largo* in B flat major, is
one of the most intimate of Handel's instrumental
pages. After seven bars of *Largo*, in which the
Concertino alternates dreamily with the *Tutti*,

two bars *adagio*, languorously drawn out, cause the reverie to glide into a sort of ecstasy,

then a *larghetto andante e piano* breathes out a tender and melancholy song.

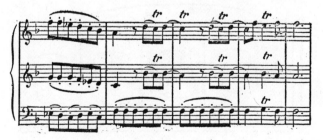

The *Largo* is resumed.   There is in this little poem a
melancholy which seems to revive Handel's personal
remembrances.—The *allegro ma non troppo* with
which it finishes is, on the contrary, of a jovial
feeling, entirely Beethovenish ; it sings joyfully as
it bounds along in well-marked three-four time, with
a *pizzicato*-like rhythm.

In the middle of this march a phrase occurs on the
two violins of the *Concertino* which is like a hymn of
reverent and tender gratitude.

The Fourth Concerto in A minor is not less intimate
with its *Larghetto affettuoso*, which ought to be
played with the *rubato, rallentando* and short pauses
—its *allegro* fugue, which spreads out and over-
shadows all by its powerful tread—and after a
Largo of antique graveness the *allegro* three-four
which finishes is the veritable last movement of the
Beethoven sonata, romantic, capricious, passionate,
and more and more unrestrained as it approaches
the end, *accelerando* nearly *prestissimo,*—inebriated.[1]

[1] See even the Third Concerto in E minor, so vivacious, with
its *Larghetto* 3-2, melancholy and serene, its *Andante* 12-8
Fugue with an elaborate theme of twirling designs which gives
the impression of the fancies of a capricious and gloomy soul,
its *Allegro* in 4-4, with a humour a little grotesque—its pic-

But one ought to know especially the Sixth
Concerto in G minor, the most celebrated of all on
account of its magnificent Musette. It opens with a
beautiful *Larghetto*, full of that melancholy which is
one of the dominant sentiments with Handel, and
one of the least observed by most people : melancholy that is, in the sense of the *Malinconia* of
Dürer, or of Beethoven—less agitated, but still
profound. We have already encountered it in the
Second, in the Third, and in the Fourth Concerto.[1]
Here it is found in an elegiac monologue, punctu-
ated by pedal points ;

turesque Polonaise on a pedal-bass, and its final *allegro ma non
troppo* of which the rhythm and unexpected modulations make
one think of certain dances in the later quartets of Beethoven.

[1] The Fifth Concerto in D major may be styled the Concerto
to St. Cecilia ; for three out of the six movements (the two first
and the beautiful final minuet) are found again in the Overture
to the little *Ode to St. Cecilia.*

then in the dialogues of the *Concertino* and of the *Tutti* responding, like the groups of the ancient classical chorus. The *allegro ma non troppo* fugue which follows it, on a twisting chromatic theme, is of the same sombre colour. But it is the lusty march of the disciplined fugue which dispels the fantastic shadows.

Then comes the *Larghetto*, three-four time in E flat major, which Handel calls a Musette, and which is one of the most delightful dreams of pastoral happiness.[1] A whole day of poetic and capricious events gradually unrolls itself over the beautiful echoing refrain,

then the movement slackens, nearly going to sleep, then presses forward again, acquiring a strong, joyous rhythm, a pulsating dance of robust youths, full of bounding life.

[1] Arnold Schering believes that the idea of this Musette was given to Handel by a *ritournelle* from Leonardo Leo's *S. Elena il Calvaroa.*

In the midst of this picture an episode, rustic and frolicsome, is introduced.

Un poco piu allegro

Then the broad subject of the Introduction recurs
with its refrain of quiet joy, nature's own smile.[1]

Such works are truly pictures in music. To
understand them it does not suffice to have quick
ears ; it is necessary to have the eyes to see, and
the heart to feel.[2]

. . . . . .

The Symphonies of the operas and oratorios of
Handel are extremely varied. Still, the Lully form
predominates.[3] This form consists, as is well

[1] The two last *allegri* conclude the work a trifle brusquely.
The order of the movements with Handel is often very surprising.
It is as though he followed the caprice of the moment.

[2] We cannot continue here the analysis of the other volumes
of Orchestral Concertos. I satisfy myself with merely enumerating
them : The 6 *Concerti grossi con due violini e violoncello di concertino obligati e due altri violini viola e basso di concerto grosso,
op.* 3, known under the name of Oboe Concertos (notwithstanding
that the oboe does not play a very prominent *rôle*), were published in 1734, and seemed to have been performed at the Wedding
of the Prince of Orange with the Princess Anne in 1733. But,
as we are told, their composition was previous to this ; for not
only do we find in the third and the fifth the reproduction of
fugues from the Clavier Pieces, but the fourth served in 1716 as
the second overture to *Amadigi*, and the first movement of the
fifth was played in 1722 in the opera *Ottone*. The form of these
Concertos, even less set than with the preceding *Concerti Grossi*,
varies from two to five movements, and their orchestration
comprises, besides the strings, two oboes, to which are occasionally added two flutes, two bassoons, the organ and the clavecin.
It is only exceptional that the oboe plays a solo part ; more
often it has to satisfy itself by reinforcing the violins.

To this volume we must add a number of other concertos,
which appeared at different times, and are brought together in
Volume XXI of the Complete Works ; especially the celebrated
Concerto of *Alexander's Feast*, written in January, 1736, of
which the style has the same massive breadth as the oratorio
itself. And four little concertos, two of which are interesting
by being youthful works, from 1703 to 1710, according to Chrysander.

[3] Handel's Overtures were so much appreciated that the
publisher Walsh issued a volume of them for the clavier (65

known, of a first slow movement, grave, pompous, and majestic, followed by a second (quick) movement, full of life, and usually in fugal style, with a return to the slow movement for conclusion. It appears in the *Almira* of 1705, and Handel uses it with variations in all the most celebrated works of his maturity, such as in the *Messiah*, and *Judas Maccabæus*, and even has recourse to it again in his last work of all, *The Triumph of Time* (1757), but he does not confine himself entirely to this form alone. The *Symphonia* of *Roderigo* (1707) adds to the Lully-like overture a *Balletto* in the Italian style, a veritable Suite of Dances : Jig, Sarabande, Matelot, Minuet, Bourrée, Minuet, Grand Passacaille. The Overture to *The Triumph of Time* of 1708 is a brilliant Concerto, where the *Concertino* and the *Grosso* converse in a most entertaining and graceful fashion. The Overture to *Il Pastor Fido*, 1712, is a Suite in eight movements. That of *Teseo*, 1713, contains two Largos, each followed by a playful movement of imitation. That of the *Passion after Brockes*, 1716, consists of a single fugued allegro,[1] which is joined to the first chorus by the link of a declamatory solo on the oboe.[2] The Overture to *Acis and Galatea*, 1720, is also a single movement. The Overture to *Giulio Cesare*, 1724, is joined on to the first chorus, which is in the form of the third movement, the Minuet. The Overture to *Atalanta*,

Overtures). A good specimen of these transcriptions is found in Volume XLVIII of the Complete Edition.

[1] Both movements are rudimentary.

[2] This device is often used by Handel to make the transition between the orchestra and the voice.

1736, has a charming sprightliness, similar to an instrumental suite for a *fête*, like the Firework Music, of which we shall speak later. The Overture to *Saul*, 1738, is a veritable Concerto for organ and orchestra, and the sonata form is adopted in the first movement.—We see then a very marked effort on the part of Handel, particularly in his youth, to vary the form of his Overture from one work to another.

Even when he uses the Lully type of Overture (and he seems to turn towards it more and more in his maturity) he transforms it by the spirit which animates it. He never allows its character to be purely decorative. He introduces therein always expressive and dramatic ideas.[1] If one cannot exactly call the splendid Overture to *Agrippina*, 1709, a Concert Overture of programme music, one cannot deny its dramatic power. The second movement bubbles with life. It is no longer an erudite *divertissement*, a movement foreign to the action, but it has a tragic character, and the response of the fugue is apparent in the severe and slightly restless subject of the first piece. For conclusion the slow movement is recalled by a solo on the oboe, which announces it out in the pathetic manner made so well known in certain *recitatives* of J. S. Bach.

[1] Scheibe, who was, with Mattheson, the greatest of German musical critics in Handel's time, states that the overture ought in its two first movements " to mark the chief character of the work " ; and in the third movement " to prepare for the first scene of the piece " (*Krit. Musikus*, 1745). Scheibe himself composed in 1738 some *Sinfonie* " which expressed to some extent the contents of the works " (*Polyeuctes, Mithridates*).

Many people have seen in the three movements[1] of
the Overture to *Esther*, 1720, a complete programme,
which Chrysander gives thus in detail : firstly, the
wickedness of Haman ; secondly, the complaints of
Israel ; thirdly, the deliverance. I will content
myself by saying that the ensemble of this symphony
is thoroughly in the colour and spirit of the tragedy
itself—but it is not possible to doubt that with the
Overture of *Deborah* and with that of *Belshazzar* that
Handel wished to work to a complete programme;
for of the four movements of the *Deborah* Overture,
the second is repeated later on as the Chorus of the
Israelites, and the fourth as the Chorus of Baal's
priests. Thus in his very first pages he places in

[1] *Andante, larghetto, allegro* (fugue).

miniature in the Overture the duality of the nations, whose antagonism forms the subject of the drama.[1] It seems also true that the Overture to *Belshazzar* aims at painting the orgy of the feast of Sesach, and the apparition of the Divine Hand which wrote the mystic words of fire on the wall. In every case dramatic intentions are very evident ; by the three repeats ; the interrupted flow of the orchestra is intersected by three short chords, *piano;* and, then after the sudden silence, three bars of solemn and soft music are heard like a religious song.[2]

[1] Only whereas a modern composer would not have omitted the opportunity of exposing his programme in an organic manner (by presenting turn by turn the two rival themes, then by bringing them into conflict, and finally terminating with the triumph of Israel's theme), Handel contents himself in exposing the two subjects without seeking to establish any further sequence. If he finishes his overture with the theme of Baal, it is because it is a gigue movement, and because the gigue serves well there for concluding ; and because Israel's song being an *adagio* is better placed as the second movement. It is such architectural considerations which guide him rather than dramatic ones. It is the same with nearly all the symphonies of the eighteenth century. In the same manner even Beethoven in his *Eroica* symphony allows his hero to die and be buried in the second movement, and then celebrates his acts and his triumphs in the third and fourth movements.

[2] Amongst the other overtures, which have the character of introduction to the work proper, I will mention the Overture to *Athalie*, which is in perfect accordance with the tragedy ;—that of *Acis and Galatea*, which is a Pastoral Symphony evoking the Pagan life of nature ;—that of the *Occasional Oratorio*, a warlike

overture with two marches, trumpet calls, and a Prayer of
distress. There is also the outline of a programme in the Overture
to *Judas Maccabæus*, of which the first movement is related to
the Funeral Scene which opens the first act, and of which the
second movement (Fugue) is connected with one of the warlike
choruses of Act I.

The Overture of *Riccardo I* (1727), in two movements, contains a tempest in music painted in a powerful and poetic

We now come to our last class of Handel's instrumental music, to which historians have given far too little attention, and in which Handel shows himself a precursor, and at the same time a model. I refer to the open-air music.

This took a prominent place in the English life. The environs of London were full of gardens, where, Pepys tells us, " vocal and instrumental concerts vied with the voices of the birds." Concerts were given at Vauxhall ; at South Lambeth Palace on the Thames ; at Ranelagh, near Chelsea, about two miles from the city ; at Marylebone Garden ; and Handel was always welcome there. From 1738 the proprietor of Vauxhall, Jonathan Tyer, erected in its gardens a statue of Handel, and this was hardly done when the *Concerti Grossi* became the favourite pieces at the concerts of Marylebone, Vauxhall, and Ranelagh. Burney tells us that he often heard them played by numerous orchestras. Handel wrote pieces especially intended for these garden concerts. Generally speaking, he attached little importance to them. They were little symphonies or unpretentious dances, like the Hornpipe, composed for the concert at Vauxhall in 1740.[1] An anecdote related by Pohl and also by Chrysander, shows

manner, which opens the first act after the manner of the Tempest in *Iphigénie en Tauride*, and on the last rumblings of which the dialogue between the heroes commences.

Finally one finds occasionally in the course of the works some other *Sinfonie* which have a dramatic character. The most striking is that which opens the third act of the *Choice of Hercules*. It depicts turn by turn the fury of Hercules and the sad force of Destiny which weighs down on his soul.

[1] Volume XLVIII of the Complete Works.

Handel pleasantly engaged on this music, which gave him no trouble at all.

But he composed on these lines some works tending towards a much vaster scale : from 1715 or 1717 the famous Water Music, written for the royal procession of barges on the Thames,[1] and the Fire-work Music made to illustrate the firework display given in Green Park on April 27, 1749, in celebration of the Peace of Aix-la-Chapelle.[2]

The Water Music has a grand Serenade in the form of a suite comprising more than twenty move-ments. It opens with a pompous Opera-overture ;

[1] The work was an immediate success. A first Edition very incorrect and incomplete was published in London about 1720, by Walsh. Arrangements for harpsichord with variations by Geminiani were also published. Both the Water Music and the Firework Music are published in Volume XLVII of the Complete Edition.

[2] One may add to these monumental pieces the *Sinfonie diverse* (pp. 140–143 of Vol. XLVIII) and the Concerto in F major in the form of an Overture and Suite (pp. 68–100, *ibid.*), but particularly the 3 *Concerti für grosses Orchester* and the 2 *Concerti a due cori* of Vol. XLVII. The *Concerti für grosses Orchester* have been, so to speak, the sketch books for the Water Music and for the Firework Music. The first Concerto dates from about 1715, and furnished two movements for the Water Music. It is written for two horns, two oboes, bassoon, two violins, violas and bass. The second Concerto in F major (for four horns, two oboes, bassoons, two violins, violas, cellos, basses and organ) ; and the third Concerto in D major (for two trumpets, four horns, drums, two oboes, bassoons, two violins, violas, cellos, organ) contains already nearly all the Firework Music with a less important orchestra, but with the Organ in addition.

The two Concertos for two horns (*Concerti a due cori*) were made from the important choruses of the Oratorios transcribed for double orchestra—ten orchestral parts for the first group, twelve for the second (four horns, eight oboes, bassoons, etc.). Thus the appearance of God in *Esther :* " Jehovah crowned in glory bright," and the connected chorus : " He comes to end our woes." There are there colossal dialogues between the two orchestras.

then come some dialogues, with echoes of horns and drums, where the brass and the rest of the orchestra, which are arranged in two sections, respond. Then follow happy and soothing songs, dances, a Bourrée, a Hornpipe, Minuets, popular songs, which alternate and contrast with the joyful and powerful fanfares. The orchestra is very nearly the same as in his usual symphonies, except that considerable importance is given to the brass. One even finds in this work certain pieces written in the chamber-music style, or in the theatrical manner.

With the Firework Music the character of open-air music is even more definitely asserted, quite as much by the broad style of the piece as by the orchestration, which is confined entirely to the wind instruments.[1] The composition is divided into two parts : an Overture which was to be played before the grand firework display, and a number of little pieces to be played during the display, and which corresponded to certain allegorical set pieces. The Overture is a sort of stately march in D major, and has some resemblance to the Overture of the *Ritterballet* (Huntsman's Dance) of Beethoven, and which is, like it, joyful, equestrian, and very

[1] The autograph MS., published in XLVII of the Complete Edition, contains: 2 parts for trumpets with 3 trumpets to a part (*i.e.* 6 trumpets) ; 3 *Prinzipali* (low trumpets) ; 3 drums ; 3 parts for horns with 3 to a part (*i.e.* 9 Horns) ; 3 parts for oboes with 12 for the first part, 8 for the second and 4 for the third (*i.e.* 24 oboes) ; 2 parts for bassoons with 8 for the first and 4 for the second (*i.e.* 12 bassoons). Total, 70 wind instruments. There were about 100 players for the performance on April 27, 1749.

Later on, Handel reproduced the work for concert use by adding the string orchestra to it.

sonorous. The shorter movements comprise a
Bourrée, a *Largo a la Siciliana*, entitled *Peace*,[1] of a
beautiful heroic grace, which lulls itself to sleep ;
a very sprightly *Allegro* entitled *The Rejoicing*, and
two Minuets for conclusion. It is an interesting
work for the organisers of our popular *fêtes* and open-
air spectacles to study.[2] If we have said that after
1740 Handel wrote hardly any other instrumental
music than the Firework Music, and the two
monumental concertos, *a due cori* (for two horns)
we have the feeling that the last evolution of his
thought and instrumental style led him in the
direction of music conceived for great masses, wide
spaces, and huge audiences. He had always in
him a popular vein of thought. I immediately
call to mind the many popular inspirations with
which his memory was stored, and which vivify
the pages of his oratorios. His art, which renewed itself perpetually at this rustic source,
had in his time an astonishing popularity. Certain
airs from *Ottone, Scipione, Arianna, Berenice*, and
such other of his operas, were circulated and
vulgarised not only in England,[3] but abroad, and

---

[1] Written for 9 horns in three sections, 24 oboes in two sections,
and 12 bassoons.

[2] It would not be difficult to add other analogous works by
Handel and Beethoven. There exists a fine repertoire of popular
classical music for open-air *fêtes*. But, nevertheless, it is completely disregarded.

[3] The Gavotte theme from the Overture to *Ottone* was played
all over England and on all kinds of instruments, " even on the
pan's-pipes of the perambulating jugglers." It was found even
at the end of the eighteenth century as a French vaudeville air.
(see the *Anthologie françoise ou Chansons choisies*, published by
Monnet, in 1765, Vol. I, p. 286). The March from *Scipio*, as also

even in France (generally so unyielding to outside influences).[1]

It is not only of this popularity, a little banal, of which I wish to speak, which one could not ignore—for it is only a stupid pride and a small heart which denies great value to the art which pleases humble people ;—what I wish to notice chiefly in the popular character of Handel's music is that it is always truly conceived for the people, and not for an *élite dilettanti*, as was the French Opera between Lully and Gluck. Without ever departing from his sovereign ideas of beautiful form, in which he gave no concession to the crowd, he reproduced in a language immediately " under-

that from *Rinaldo*, served during half a century for the Parade of the Life Guards. The minuets and overtures from *Arianna* and Berenice had a long popularity. One sees in the English novels of the time (especially in Fielding's *Tom Jones*) to what an extent Handel's music had permeated English country life, even from the small country squires to the county magnates, so absolutely cut off as they were from *all* artistic influences.

[1] Paul Marie Masson has noticed that about the date of 1716, in a volume of *Recueil d'airs serieux et à boire* (Bibl. Nat. Vm. 549), an *Aria del Signor Inden* (sic), " *air ajouté au ballet de l'Europe Galante.*" The *Meslanges de musique latine, françoise et italienne* of Ballard (in 1728), contains amongst the Italian airs *Arie de Signor Endel* (p. 61). All the airs of the *Chasse du cerf* by Sere de Rieux (1734) are Handel airs adapted to French words. An article by Michel Brenet, *La librairie musicale en France de* 1653 *à* 1790, *d'après les registres de priviléges* (*Sammelbände I.M.G.*, 1907) gives a series of French Editions of Handel from 1736, 1739, 1749, 1751, 1765. In 1736 and in 1743 in *Concerts Spirituels* some of his airs and his *Concerti Grossi* were given (Brenet : *Les Concerts en France sous l'ancien régime*, 1900). A number of his airs were arranged for the flute by Blavet in his three *Receuils de pièces, petits airs, brunettes, minuets, etc., accommodés pour les flutes traversières, violins, etc.*, which appeared between 1740 and 1750. Handel was so well known in Paris that they sold his portrait there in 1739. (See a tradesman's advertisement in the *Mercure de France*, June, 1739, Vol. II, page 1384.)

standed of the people " those feelings in which all
could share. This genial improvisor, compelled
during the whole of his life (a half-century of
creative power) to address from the stage a mixed
public, for whom it was necessary to understand
immediately, was like the orators of old, who had
the cult of style and instinct for immediate and vital
effect. Our epoch has lost the feeling of this type
of art and men: pure artists who speak *to* the
people and *for* the people, not for themselves or for
their confrères. To-day the pure artists lock themselves within themselves, and those who speak to
the people are most often mountebanks. The free
England of the nineteenth century was in a certain
measure related to the Roman republic, and indeed
Handel's eloquence was not without relation to
that of the epic orators, who sustained in the form
their highly finished and passionate discourses, who
left their mark on the shuddering crowd of loiterers.
This eloquence did on occasion actually thrust itself
into the soul of the nation as in the days of the
Jacobite invasion, where *Judas Maccabæus* incar-
nated the public feeling. In the first performances
of *Israel in Egypt* some of the auditors praised the
heroic virtues of this music, which could raise up
the populace and lead armies to victory.

By this power of popular appeal, as by all the
other aspects of his genius, Handel was in the
robust line of Cavalli and of Gluck, but he surpassed
them.   Alone, Beethoven has walked in these
broader paths, and followed along the road which
Handel had opened.

LIST OF HANDEL'S WORKS

I. OPERAS

IN chronological order, with the dates and places of the first performance.

(The figures in brackets refer to the number of the Volume in the Complete Edition of Handel's Works.)

1. *Almira* (55)	. . .	Hamburg,	1705.
2. *Nero* (lost)	. . .	,,	1705.
3. *Florinda* (lost)	. .	,, about	1706.
4. *Daphne* (lost)	. . .	,, about	1706.
5. *Roderigo* (56)	. . . .	Florence,	1707.
6. *Agrippina* (57)	. . .	Venice,	1708.
7. *Rinaldo* (58)	. . . .	London,	1711.
8. *Il Pastor Fido* (59)	. . .	,,	1712.
9. *Teseo* (60)	. . . .	,,	1713.
10. *Silla* (61). Never performed in public (probably privately performed at Canons).			
11. *Amadigi* (62)	. . . .	London,	1715.
12. *Radamisto* (63)	. . .	,,	1720.
(There are three versions.)			
13. *Muzio Scævola* (64)	. . .	,,	1721.
14. *Floridante* (65)	. . .	,,	1721.
15. *Ottone* (66)	. . . .	,,	1723.
16. *Flavio* (67)	. . . .	,,	1723.
17. *Giulio Cesare* (68)	. . .	,,	1724.
18. *Tamerlano* (69)	. . .	,,	1724.

19. *Rodelinda* (70)   .   .   .   London, 1725.
20. *Scipione* (71) .   .   .   .   ,,   1726.
21. *Alessandro* (72)   .   .   .   ,,   1726.
22. *Admeto* (73) .   .   .   .   ,,   1727.
23. *Riccardo Primo, Re d'Inghilterra*   ,,   1727.
24. *Siroe* (75)   .   .   .   .   ,,   1728.
25. *Tolomeo, Re d'Egitto* (76)   .   ,,   1728.
26. *Lotario* (77) .   .   .   .   ,,   1729.
27. *Partenope* (78)   .   .   .   ,,   1730.
28. *Rinaldo* (new version) (58)   .   ,,   1731.
29. *Poro* (79)   .   .   .   .   ,,   1731.
30. *Ezio* (80)   .   .   .   .   ,,   1732.
31. *Sosarme* (81) .   .   .   .   ,,   1732.
32. *Orlando* (82) .   .   .   .   ,,   1733.
33. *Arianna* (83) .   .   .   .   ,,   1734.
34. *Terpsichore* (84).
35. *Ariodante* (85)   .   .   .   ,,   1735.
36. *Alcina* (86)   .   .   .   .   ,,   1735.
37. *Atalanta* (87) .   .   .   .   ,,   1736.
38. *Giustino* (88) .   .   .   .   ,,   1737.
39. *Arminio* (89) .   .   .   .   ,,   1737.
40. *Berenice* (90) .   .   .   .   ,,   1737.
41. *Faramondo* (91)   .   .   .   ,,   1738.
42. *Serse* (92)   .   .   .   .   ,,   1738.
43. *Imeneo* (93)   .   .   .   .   ,,   1740.
44. *Deidamia* (94) .   .   .   .   ,,   1741.
45. *Jupiter in Argos* (MS. Fitzwilliam Museum, Cambridge. Advertised but never performed), 1739.
46. *Tito.* Unperformed and unpublished.
47. *Alfonso Imo.* Unperformed and unpublished.
48. *Flavio Olibrio.* Unperformed and unpublished.
49. *Honorius.* Unperformed and unpublished.
50. An unnamed opera (MS. Fitzwilliam Museum).
51. Eleven Pasticcios, arranged at various times between 1730 and 1747.

II. Oratorios

1. *Passion according to St. John* (9) .	Hamburg,	1704.
2. *Resurrezione* (32) . . .	Rome,	1708.
3. *Il Trionfo del Tempo* (24) . .	,,	1708.
4. *The Passion of Christ* (15) . .	Hamburg,	1717.
5. *Esther* (First Version) . ˙.	Canons,	1720.
6. *Esther* (Second Version)		
	King's Theatre, London,	1733.
7. *Deborah* (29) .	King's Theatre, London,	1733.
8. *Athaliah* (5)	Oxford,	1733.
9. *Saul* (13) . .	King's Theatre, London,	1739.
10. *Israel in Egypt* (16) . ,,	,,	1739.
11. *Messiah*	Dublin,	1742.
12. *Samson* (10) . . .	Covent Garden,	1743.
13. *Joseph* (42) . . . ,,	,,	1744.
14. *Belshazzar* (19) . . .	King's Theatre,	1745.
15. *Occasional Oratorio* (43) .	Covent Garden,	1746.
16. *Judas Maccabæus* (22) . ,,	,,	1747.
17. *Joshua* (17) . . . ,,	,,	1748.
18. *Alexander Balus* (33) . . ,,	,,	1748.
19. *Solomon* (26) . . . ,,	,,	1749.
20. *Susanna* (1) . . . ,,	,,	1749.
21. *Theodora* (8) . . . ,,	,,	1750.
22. *Jephtha* (44) . . . ,,	,,	1752.
23. *Triumph of Time and Truth* (20) ,,	,,	1757.

III. Odes, Serenatas, and Occasional Pieces

1. *Acis, Galatea e Polifemo* (53) .	Naples,	1708.
2. *Birthday Ode for Queen Anne* (46a)		
	St. James' Palace,	1713.
3. *Acis and Galatea* (3) . . .	Canons,	1720.

4. *The Alchemist* . . . Covent Garden, 1732.
5. *Il Parnasso in Festa* (54) . King's Theatre, 1734.
6. *Alexander's Feast* (12) . . Covent Garden, 1736.
7. *Ode for St. Cecilia's Day* (23)

Lincoln's Inn Fields, 1739.
8. *Praise of Harmony* . ,, ,, about 1739.
9. *L'Allegro, Il Penseroso ed Il*
Moderato (6) . . Lincoln's Inn Fields, 1740.
10. *Hymen* . . . . . Dublin, 1742.
11. *Semele* (7) . . . . Covent Garden, 1744.
12. *Hercules* (4) . . . King's Theatre, 1745.
13. *Alceste* (46b). Incidental music
to play. (Never performed) 1749 or 1750.
14. *Choice of Hercules* (18). An
Interlude . . . Covent Garden, 1751.

IV. Church Music

1. *Laudate Pueri in F* . . . Halle, 1702.
2. *Dixit Dominus* (38) . . . Rome, 1707.
3. *Nisi Dominus* (38) . . Rome or Halle.
4. *Laudate Pueri in D* (38) . . Rome, 1707.
5. *Silete venti* (38) . . . . ,, 1708.
6. *Six Alleluias* (38). For voice and
harpsichord.
7. *Utrecht Te Deum and Jubilate* (31)

St. Paul's Cathedral, 1713.
8. *Te Deum in D* (37) . . . About 1714.
9. *Fifteen Chandos Anthems* (34). For
chorus, organ and orchestra . Canons, 1716–18.
10. *Te Deum in B flat* (37) . . . ,, 1716–18.
11. *Four Coronation Anthems* (14).
For seven-part chorus and large
orchestra . . Westminster Abbey, 1727.

12. *Te Deum in A* (37) . . . About 1727.
13. *O Praise the Lord, Ps. CIII.*, etc. (36). Anthem for chorus and orchestra.
14. *Wedding Anthem, Ps. XLV.*, etc. (36). Eight-part chorus, solos, orchestra, and organ
  Wedding of Princess Anne, 1734.
15. *Wedding Anthem, Ps. LXVIII.*, etc. Chorus, solos, and orchestra
  Wedding of the Prince of Wales, 1736.
16. *Funeral Anthem* (11) Death of Queen Caroline, 1737.
17. *Dettingen Te Deum* (25) . . . 1743.
18. *Dettingen Anthem, Ps. X. and XI.*, etc. (36) . . . . . . 1743.
19. *Foundling Hospital Anthem, Ps. XLI.*, etc. (36) . . . . 1749.
20. Three Hymns. MS. in Fitzwilliam Museum. Words by the Rev. C. Wesley. "Sinners, obey the Gospel word," "O Love divine, how sweet thou art," "Rejoice, the Lord is King."

V. Vocal Chamber Music

1. Seventy-two Solo Cantatas for one or two voices with instruments (52 a, b, c). Italian. No. 8 is English; No. 18 is Spanish with guitar accompaniment.
2. Twenty-two Italian Duets and two Trios with harpsichord and violoncello (32).
3. Seven Italian Sonatas. Unpublished. MSS. in Fitzwilliam Museum.

VI. Instrumental Music

1. Six Sonatas for two oboes with
   thorough-bass for harpsichord (73)   .   1696.
2. Sonata for viola - da - gamba and
   cembalo concertata in C (48) . Hamburg, 1705.
3. *Klavierbuch aus der Jugendzeit* (48)   1710.
4. Three Sonatas for flute and harpsichord (48)   .   Probably Hanover, about 1710.
5. Water Music (47)   .   .   .   1715.
6. *Suites de pièces pour clavecin* (2) . Published 1720.
7. Fifteen Solos for a German flute,
   oboe or violin, with a thorough-
   bass for harpsichord or bass
   violin (27)   .   .   .   .   .   1724.
8. Six Concertos (21), Op. 3. *Concerti grossi con due violini e
   violoncello di concertino e due
   altri violini, viola e basso di
   concerto grosso ad arbitrio,*
   known as the Oboe Concertos . Walsh, 1729.
9. Nine Sonatas or Trios for two
   violins, flutes, or oboes, with a
   thorough-bass for harpsichord
   or violoncello, Op. 2 (27)   .   . Walsh, 1733.
10. *Suites de pièces pour clavecin* (2).
    Second volume pilfered by
    Walsh in 1733.
11. *Pièces pour clavecin* (2).   Five
    pieces Witvogel in Amsterdam,
    1733.   Several clavecin pieces
    still remain in MS. at Buckingham
    Palace and Fitzwilliam Museum.

12. Overture for the pasticcio *Oreste* (48) . . . . . . 1734.
13. Six "Fugues or Voluntaries for the organ or harpsichord," Op. 3a (2) . . . . . Walsh, 1735.
14. Overture in G minor for the pasticcio *Alessandro Severo* (48) . . 1738.
15. Six Organ Concertos, Op. 4 (48) . Walsh, 1738.
16. Seven Sonatas or Trios for two violins or German flutes, with a thorough-bass for the harpsichord or violoncello, Op. 5 (27) . Walsh, 1739.
17. Hornpipe, composed for the concert at Vauxhall (48). For strings in three parts . . . 1740.
18. Six Concertos for organ arranged by Walsh from the Orchestral Concertos . . . . . . 1740.
19. Twelve Grand Concertos, Op. 6a (30). For strings only, in seven parts . . . . Walsh, 1740.
20. *Pièces pour le clavecin* (2) . . Cluer, 1742.
21. Forest Music (47) . . . . 1742.
22. Fire Music (47) . . . . . 1749.
23. Concerto for two organs and orchestra in D minor (48). Movement only exists.
24. Overture in B minor (48). Adapted by Walsh from the Overture to *Trionfo del Tempo*.
25. Organ Concerto in D minor (48). Two movements.
26. Organ Concerto in F (48).
27. Partita in A (48).
28. Six little Fugues. (Dubious.)
29. Concerto for trumpets and horns.

30. Concerto for horns and side-drums.
31. *Sinfonie diverse* (48). Eight short pieces for orchestral instruments.
32. Overture in five movements (incomplete) for two clarionets and corno di caccia. MS. in Fitzwilliam Museum.

*   *   *

The COMPLETE HANDEL EDITION contains as supplements several volumes of works by various Italian and German composers, which Handel has utilised in his compositions, namely:—

1. *Magnificat* said to be by Erba.
2. *Te deum* said to be by Vrio.
3. *Serenata* by Stradella.
4. *Duetti* by Clari.
5. *Componimenti musicali* by G. Muffat.
6. *Octavia* by Reinhard Keiser.

BIBLIOGRAPHY

FRIEDRICH CHRYSANDER, *G. F. Handel.* 3 vols., 1858-67, Leipzig.

(The name of Chrysander ought to be attached permanently to that of Handel, for his life was entirely devoted to him. It was he who founded in 1856, with Gervinus, the GERMAN HANDEL SOCIETY and who accomplished nearly the whole of the Complete Edition of the Works of Handel in one hundred volumes by himself alone. His biography is a monument of science and devotion comparable with Philipp Spitta's *J. S. Bach* and Otto Jahn's *Mozart.* Unfortunately the work remained unfinished : it stopped at the year 1740. Max Seiffert completed it.

SCHOELCHER, *The Life of Handel.* 1857.

(Schoelcher's works, anterior to those of Chrysander, are valuable on account of their collection of documents rather than that of the general laying out of the works. As we have seen, the priceless collection of these documents is housed at the Paris Conservatoire.)

HERMANN KRETZSCHMAR, *Georg Friedrich Handel* (published in the *Sammlung musikalischer Vorträge* by Paul Graf Waldersee).

FRITZ VOLBACH, *Georg-Friedrich Hændel* (Collection : *Harmonie.* 1898, Berlin).

(These two last works are excellent little *résumés* of the life and works of Handel.)

J. A. Fuller-Maitland, *The Age of Bach and Handel* (The Oxford History of Music, Vol. IV). 1902, Oxford.

R. A. Streatfeild, *Handel.* 1909, London.
(This book is one of the first in England which has freed the figure of Handel from the false mass of moralising and teaching under which the author of the *Messiah* was buried. He shows the richness and freedom of Handel's work and rectifies several points in the German biographies.)

Adimolo, *G. F. Handel in Italia.*

Sedley Taylor, *The Indebtedness of Handel to Works by other Composers.* 1906, Cambridge.

P. Robinson, *Handel and his Orbit.* 1908, London.
(These two last books are concerned with the question of Handel's plagiarisms.)

F. Volbach, *Die Praxis der Hændel-Aufführung*, 1889. Thesis for Doctorate.
(On the Orchestra of Handel.)

Hugo Goldschmidt, *Die Lehre von der vocalen Ornamentik.* 1907.
(On the vocal execution of Handel's works, and particularly on the question of Handel's ornaments. This matter has been the subject of numerous discussions in the numbers of the *International Musical Gazette*, especially by Max Seiffert.)

Weitzmann, *Geschichte der Klaviermusik*, Vol. I, 1899 (continued and completed by Seiffert and Fleischer).
(For the Clavier Works of Handel.)

Ernest David, *Handel.* 1884.

Camille Bellaigue, *Les Époques de la Musique*, Vol. I, 1909.

For readers desirous of consulting the sources of the biographies of Handel, the most interesting works written by his contempories are :

JOHANN MATTHESON, *Hændel* (in his *Ehrenpforte,* 1740).

MAINWARING, *Memoirs of the Life of the late G. F. Handel.* London, 1760. (Translated into German with annotations by Mattheson, 1761 ; into French by Arnaud and Suard in 1778.)

BURNEY, *Commemoration of Handel.* London, 1785.

HAWKINS, *General History of Music.* London, 1788.

W. COXE, *Anecdotes of G. F. Handel and Smith.* London, 1799.

INDEX